CURTMANTLE

CHRISTOPHER FRY

CURTMANTLE

A Play

Second Edition

LONDON

OXFORD UNIVERSITY PRESS

NEW YORK   TORONTO

1965

Oxford University Press, Amen House, London, E.C.4

GLASGOW NEW YORK TORONTO MELBOURNE WELLINGTON
BOMBAY CALCUTTA MADRAS KARACHI LAHORE DACCA
CAPE TOWN SALISBURY NAIROBI IBADAN ACCRA
KUALA LUMPUR HONG KONG

First published 1961
Second edition 1965

PRINTED IN GREAT BRITAIN

To

JOHN AND NANCY FRY

The play was first produced on 1 March 1961 at the state opening of the Stadsschouwburg, Tilburg, Holland, by the Ensemble Company, directed by Karl Guttmann

World première in English at the Edinburgh Festival, 4 September 1962

London première at the Aldwych Theatre, 6 October 1962, with the following cast:

William Marshal	ROY DOTRICE
Barber	JOHN HUSSEY
Wife	SUSAN ENGEL
Juggler	ROBERT JENNINGS
Huckster	KEN WYNNE
Blae	PATSY BYRNE
A man looking for justice	TREVOR MARTIN
Eleanor	MAXINE AUDLEY
Henry	DEREK GODFREY
Becket	ALAN DOBIE
Cleric	DONALD LAYNE-SMITH
Gilbert Foliot	JOHN NETTLETON
Earl of Leicester	PAUL DAWKINS
Christ Church monks	KEN WYNNE JOHN HUSSEY
Young Henry Richard Geoffrey } *the King's sons* John	ROGER CROUCHER DAVID BUCK IAN MCCULLOCH MARTIN NORTON
Roger, *the King's son by Blae*	BRIAN SMITH
Messenger	SHAUN CURRY
Courtiers at Poitou	DARRYL KAVANN EDWARD ARGENT
Constance, *Geoffrey's wife*	SUSAN ENGEL
Margaret, *Young Henry's wife*	MARIAN DIAMOND
Captain	TREVOR MARTIN
Philip of France	PETER MCENERY
Old woman	MADOLINE THOMAS
Refugees	PAUL DAWKINS ROY MARSDEN CHERRY MORRIS IAN RICKETTS

Bishops: EDWARD ARGENT, TERENCE GREENIDGE, ROBERT JENNINGS, HENRY KNOWLES

Courtiers and Soldiers: MARGARETA BOURDIN, IMOGEN HASSALL, CAROLINE HUNT, CAROLINE MAUD, MARK MOSS, KENNETH RATCLIFFE, STUART RICHMAN, LESLIE SOUTHWICK

Directed by STUART BURGE

FOREWORD

HENRY PLANTAGENET was born in 1133, the son of Matilda (daughter of Henry I) and Geoffrey Plantagenet, Count of Anjou. During his boyhood England was suffering an eight-year-long agony of civil war, fought between his mother and Stephen of Blois. At the age of twenty-one he was King, and the wealthiest ruler in Europe. At fifty-six he was dead, the sword of State pawned, his heart broken. But 'he had laid the foundations of the English Common Law, upon which succeeding generations would build. Changes in the design would arise, but its main outlines would not be altered.'[1]

Between these two dates there is a seething cauldron of events, conflicts, purposes, errors, brilliance, human endurance, and human suffering, which could provide, in those thirty-five years, all that we need for a lifetime's study and contemplation of mankind. No single play could contain more than a splash from the brew. What to use and what to lose out of this feverish concentration of life? How far should fidelity to historical events be sacrificed to suit the theatre?

If a playwright is rash enough to treat real events at all, he has to accept a double responsibility: to drag out of the sea of detail a story simple enough to be understood by people who knew nothing about it before; and to do so without distorting the material he has chosen to use. Otherwise let him invent his characters, let him go to Ruritania for his history.

To try to re-create what has taken place in this world (or, indeed, to write about life at all) is to be faced by the task of putting a shape on almost limitless complexity. The necessity for the shaping—for 'making a play of it'—is inherent in us, because pattern and balance

[1] Winston Churchill, *The History of the English-speaking Peoples*, Vol. I.

are pervading facts of the universe. It is tempting to make a misleading simplification. In the absence of any other household-god, simplification becomes a gross superstition. It gives us the security of 'knowing', of being at home in events. We even call it reality, or getting down to the truth. But everything that we ignored remains to confute us.

I can't pretend that the play which follows has solved the problems, but consideration of them has dictated the way it should go. Though it follows chronology, it is not a chronicle play. The form it takes is one of memory and contemplation. The stage is William Marshal's mind, as though he were remembering the life of Henry; and the deviations from historical accuracy are on the whole no greater than might occur in a man's memory. The episodes are telescoped, but nothing in the play is entirely invented. Even the incident of the old woman and her feather-bed is on record.

But because, as far as I could, I have tried to do away with time and place, and to convey thirty years in one almost uninterrupted action, a few manipulations of fact have crept in. For instance, when Henry gives his age as twenty-nine, it is not the age he was at that precise point in the story (he was twenty-five), but the age he was two pages later, when he offers Canterbury to Becket. Then, also, he didn't die at Le Mans; he went on to make the desperate ride which he only plans in the play, and the meeting with Philip and Richard took place at Colombières. Nor did he die on the old woman's feather mattress, but on a bed at Chinon. The final episode, which I give to the townspeople of Le Mans, rightly belongs to Henry's own servants.

The character of Roger is a combination of two illegitimate sons, one born of a prostitute, and another who became Geoffrey the Chancellor. I renamed him to avoid the confusion of having two characters called Geoffrey.

The play has two themes: one a progression towards a portrait of Henry, a search for his reality, moving through versions of

'Where is the King?' to the unresolved close of 'He was dead when they came to him'. The other theme is Law, or rather the interplay of different laws: civil, canon, moral, aesthetic, and the laws of God; and how they belong and do not belong to each other.

It adds up to no more than a sketch of Henry. Just as the thirty-five years of his reign contain a concentration of the human condition, so his character covers a vast field of human nature. He was simple and royal (his nickname of 'Curtmantle' derived from the plain short cloak he wore), direct and paradoxical, compassionate and hard, a man of intellect, a man of action, God-fearing, superstitious, blasphemous, far-seeing, short-sighted, affectionate, lustful, patient, volcanic, humble, overriding. It is difficult to think of any facet of man which at some time he didn't demonstrate, except chastity and sloth.

My starting place was Mrs. J. R. Green's *Henry the Second*. Among the other books I read on the period, I am particularly indebted to Amy Kelly's *Eleanor of Aquitaine*.

C. F.

May 1961

NOTE TO THE SECOND EDITION

DURING the rehearsals for the English production I made a certain number of minor textual alterations, and added two short scenes: the conversation between the two monks about Becket's escape from England, and the scene between Henry, Roger, and Richard, before we come to Le Mans. This was a considerably condensed version of a scene which was played in the Dutch production.

After the performances at the Edinburgh Festival I made some more small changes, and reshaped those pages which extend from the news of the birth of Philip of France, to Richard's song after the coronation. I also rehandled the scene of Eleanor's court at Poitou.

I have begun both the Prologue and Act III with some words from Marshal, to establish him as the memory in which the action of the play takes place.

For the English production I reduced the length of the Prologue by half, but I have left it in its full form in the printed text. An audience hasn't a reader's privilege of being able to skip at will.

C. F.

1965

CHARACTERS

(in order of their appearance)

BARBER
WIFE
JUGGLER
HUCKSTER
BLAE
ANESTY
ELEANOR
WILLIAM MARSHAL
HENRY
BECKET
CLERIC
GILBERT FOLIOT
EARL OF LEICESTER
YOUNG HENRY, *the King's Son*
RICHARD ⎫
GEOFFREY ⎬ *his brothers*
JOHN ⎭
ROGER
MESSENGER
BECKET'S CROSS-BEARER
CONSTANCE, *Geoffrey's wife*
MARGARET, *Young Henry's wife*
CAPTAIN
PHILIP OF FRANCE
OLD WOMAN
FOUR REFUGEES
BISHOPS, MONKS, COURTIERS, SOLDIERS

PROLOGUE

BARBER

WIFE

JUGGLER

HUCKSTER

BLAE

ANESTY

ACT ONE

ELEANOR

WILLIAM MARSHAL

HENRY

BECKET

CLERIC

GILBERT FOLIOT

PROLOGUE

MARSHAL. Memory is not so harsh as the experience. Who can
recall now the full devastation of the time when young Henry
Plantagenet first came into his Kingdom? Henry Curtmantle, we
sometimes called him, with his cloak as short as his need for
sleep. His energy was like creation itself; he was giving form to
England's chaos, an England that, after eight years of civil war,
had no trade, no law, no conscience. Up and down the land he
went, sparing neither himself nor us who were hauled along after
him. Order was being born out of the sweat of those days and
nights: a time of pugnacious reality, that still plays in my mind—
beginning and ending, as it did in his thoughts also, with the
people he governed.

*On the edge of an improvised encampment. Cart shafts hung with
clothes to make sleeping quarters. A wind is blowing. A man, a*
HUCKSTER, *is beating a drum. The King's* BARBER *and his*
WIFE *shouting to each other above the wind and the drumming.
Enter through the shadows a third man, a* JUGGLER.

BARBER. We're on the edge of the marsh. It's the noise of the frogs
you can hear!

WIFE. What is it?

BARBER. The croaking of frogs!

JUGGLER. Men are getting rough where I've just come from.

BARBER. Who's beating the drum?

JUGGLER. Shine the lantern over here, will you? I've got blood
coming out of me.

BARBER [*moving towards the* HUCKSTER]. Give us a chance to sleep, what's the matter with you?

HUCKSTER. I'm discouraging away the evils of the night.

BARBER. Discourage that drum for one.

JUGGLER. Bring us the light. The clumsy, excitable sons of bitches have dug a hole in me.

BARBER. What's the matter?

JUGGLER. They've gone mad up in front there, arguing over who has the best right to accommodation. I was trying to get past 'em, and got stuck on a knife. Hold the light still.

BARBER. Anyway, you won't die of it.

JUGGLER. The clumsy, excitable sons of bitches!

HUCKSTER. I'd be better off in London, I'll tell you that. If it rains on us now—*mercy domine*! You have to be like iron to follow the King.

JUGGLER. Whose bucket of water?

BLAE [*emerging from the dark*]. It's mine, dearie. Come on here; I'll cure you.

JUGGLER. I can manage, love.

WIFE. So she's learnt to cure 'em as well; very useful, I should think.

BLAE. I learn not to listen, see, Jack, I say nothing.

WIFE. If my husband was anything of a man, he would see I was sleeping somewhere better than this.

BARBER. She tells me a man would have elbowed his way up to the front and made himself known. 'I'm the King's barber', she says a man would have said, 'and you can all go and hook yourselves up on a bush'.

JUGGLER. I wouldn't be a man on those terms, Barber. Look what I got, and I was only walking past them.

[2]

WIFE. It sounds like they're slaughtering rats.

JUGGLER. It's plain vicious brawling. It doesn't hurt the King to change his mind where he's going to. No harm to him to land us up ten miles from no place; and no daylight, either, to see where to spit. And a dirty night coming up on the wind. He's lying well out of the weather in the farmhouse, with ten or twelve of the best of the lords lying alongside him. But when you've had that, there's an old splay-footed barn, and then you're down to the cow-house and the pigsties; and that's where the trouble started. Who's to have the accommodation? Who's to have the honour and precedence to lie down in the muck in the pigsty? That's the beginning of the argument, rising up to blaspheming oratory, then shouldering and shoving, and simple Jack has to go and pass them just when they fetch out their damned cutlery.

[A yell is heard above the brawling.

BARBER. There's somebody accommodated.

WIFE. We're better off where we are.

BARBER. That's what I said.

HUCKSTER. What sort of a world is it, Jesus hear me? You'd think when a man goes travelling with the King's Court he'd make a fortune for himself. But what's the outcome of it? Grinding forward, day after day, through miles of mud, and find your night's lodging in a filthy swamp.

BARBER. You can tell yourself it's a great benefit to the kingdom. That's the outcome of it. Law and order is the outcome. Haven't you got a memory for the smoke and ruin this land was? Mad, and murderous, and lawless, bleeding away like raw meat.

HUCKSTER. I can have more of that at home in my own bed.

JUGGLER. What's here? There's a light coming.

WIFE. See it? Yes, look, there it is.

[3]

BARBER. Who else is out in the night, looking for somewhere to sleep?

HUCKSTER. That's the marshes down there. That's not an ordinary light. That leads you off to sink over your ears in a mucky death. *[He nervously beats on the drum.*

BARBER. Give that a rest; give it up.

JUGGLER. Picking his way, the poor bloody man. We'll hollow at him.

BARBER. He's hollowing himself. [*To the* HUCKSTER.] Quiet, for God's sake!—Let's hear what he says.

    [RICHARD ANESTY, *the traveller, calls from a short distance.*

ANESTY. Who's there to hear me?

JUGGLER. Any number.

ANESTY. Have I caught up with the King?

JUGGLER. You're on the verge of him. Struggle on.

BARBER. Who would come to this place looking for the King, where we don't know where we are ourselves?

WIFE. Where we wouldn't be if we knew better.

HUCKSTER. A hell of a valley to come and lodge in.

    [*They wait for him. Enter* RICHARD ANESTY, *his sword drawn.*

JUGGLER. Draw into the circle, friend. We aren't quarrelsome.

ANESTY. God save you.

HUCKSTER. Let's hope so.

BARBER. You can save us your sword, as well.

JUGGLER. Put it by, man.

BARBER. If you think we're a lawless lot, no wonder, seeing us pitched out here in a black, spitting wind. But that's how the journey has gone, with the best of intentions. Otherwise we're decent men.

[4]

WIFE. He's the King's barber talking to you.

ANESTY. Then tell me where I can find the King.

JUGGLER. Show us your face.

ANESTY. Get me to the King.

BARBER. Steady, now, steady. What makes you think he'll see a gaunt, atrocious man rushing in on him out of the dark?

JUGGLER. Tell us your name.

ANESTY. Richard Anesty.

BARBER. What do you want with the King, Richard Anesty?

ANESTY. Simply a matter of birthright: of common justice. Where shall I find him?

BARBER. Wait, now, wait! Give us a proper explanation of yourself.

ANESTY. To satisfy the barber? So that's what I've come to. Well, the name is Anesty. My property was a fair property: was heft off me in the civil wars. It's taken five years, going through the courts, trying to get it back again. I'm sick of that particular labyrinth; it breaks the spirit. The King's the only answer. He'll see the matter set right: loves the law, hates the grabbing barony. He'll see the future gives me a world of my proper rights. Which way do I go to him?

BARBER. No way, at this hour of the night.

ANESTY. Who do you think will stop me now?

BARBER. You stay here, sir, as I say to you.

ANESTY. Not for a barber!

BARBER [*holding his arm*]. Then we'll have to keep you, for your own good!

JUGGLER [*taking the other;* ANESTY *struggles*]. Calm your soul, sir.

ANESTY. Right, when I've seen the King.

BARBER. And that's first thing in the morning. He's seeing all the

B [5]

men then who have a reasonable cause for complaining, before we move off.

BLAE. At six o'clock.

WIFE. You can believe her. She gets the accurate information always, one way and another.

ANESTY. But I'm within yards of putting my hand to him. Do you know what you're asking?

JUGGLER. Well, the time will pass easy enough if you're sleeping.

ANESTY. I've been searching for him seven weeks and two days. I've had two horses die on the road, the last an hour or so ago, three miles short of catching up with you. There was no way of knowing, from one day to the next, where the King would be.

BARBER. Right, sir. That's his whole plan and purpose. Find out the true state of the courts of law and the administration of his kingdom, is what he is after; so come up on them unawares is what he does. Thursday at Nottingham, says the itinerary. So the judges at Nottingham keep sober Monday, Tuesday, Wednesday, put off accepting any bribes till Friday, rub the dirt off their hands, and sit down to business as punctual as the light. And where is the King's majesty? The King's majesty is in Sheffield.

ANESTY. I know it very well.

JUGGLER. Well, here you are; get some sleep. The morning's not so far off. You'll have no trouble from the King if you've got a good claim.

HUCKSTER. Though you might wonder, looking at us here. He'll march us all to death to get his law and order, though I'll say this, he's sorry for you when you're dead. Concerning the foreign sailors wrecked on our coast, per example, and the killing, robbing, and stripping thereof, he wept like a sweating cistern, as we saw at Whitstable. The veins in his head stood up the size of ropes,

[6]

condemning the practices to perjury-come. So we know to be butchered if we want to be well thought of.

BARBER [*indicating the* HUCKSTER *with his head*]. A highly nervous trading kind of man, with no wide thoughts at all for the world's good.—Haven't you got a memory for the smoke and ruin this land was? Mad, and murderous, and lawless, bleeding away like raw meat!

JUGGLER. Half a lifetime of it, if you can put that out of your memory.

BARBER. Foul injustice done to good men. As this good man here himself has suffered, so he tells us.

JUGGLER. This good man here is fast asleep.

BARBER. There it is, you see: good men can sleep now, under the wisdom of King Henry.

WIFE. Under a cart, if you wouldn't mind noticing.

BARBER. The wind is taking the clouds off. There it is: times are improving.

HUCKSTER. But I'm not, Jesus hear me.

JUGGLER. Six good hours insensible. I'll enjoy that. Goodnight, friends.

[*The camp settles down to sleep. A horn begins to blow, coming nearer; shouts and a growing murmur.*

JUGGLER [*groaning*]. What's the trouble now?

HUCKSTER. Isn't there to be any night between days in this King's world, for God's sake?

BARBER. We'd better find out.

VOICE [*coming nearer*]. Break up camp, get on the road!

HUCKSTER. They've gone out of their minds.

VOICE. Break up camp!

WIFE. What do they mean? Now? In the night?

[7]

VOICE. The King's in the saddle! Hurry yourselves! We're making for Kettering!

JUGGLER. What fool drunk has started this?

BARBER [*returning from inquiry*]. The camp's breaking up. We've got to move.

WIFE. Kettering!

JUGGLER. That means the best part of twenty miles before morning.

HUCKSTER. If a man can't have his lawful sleep, to hell with the law.

[*The camp is busy and noisy, the lanterns moving, the carts being wheeled away.*

BARBER [*shaking* ANESTY *as he passes him*]. Better wake up, Richard Anesty. The King has left for Kettering.

ANESTY. The King—

BARBER. The King is riding off to Kettering.

ANESTY [*struggling to his feet*]. No, no, no! It isn't light yet. You swore to me you would bring me to him in the morning.

BARBER. So we thought we would, but we're moving on.

ANESTY. You don't know what you're saying! I have to see him! He has only got to lean a moment from his saddle! What can I do? How can I go on?—Where is the King?

[*The stage empties and darkens.*

Where shall I find the King? A law that's just and merciful! Do I have to walk on for ever, looking for that?

[*He trudges after the receding noise of the wagons.*

Where is the King?

[*The wind blows in the dark, drops to a calm, and gradually the light increases on an empty hall in Westminster, no person there except the Queen,* ELEANOR, *standing alone.*

END OF PROLOGUE

ACT ONE · 1158-63

Westminster. ELEANOR. *Enter* WILLIAM MARSHAL, *grinning.*

MARSHAL. The King's arrived in the yard, ma'am, with the Chancellor.

ELEANOR. And every man in London appears to be smiling.
What is it, Marshal? Every man
Who has come in out of the street is either grinning,
Or sprawling a great hand across his mouth,
As though there were something of obscene pleasure in the world
outside.

MARSHAL. Well, possibly it might be a general feeling of success.
As far as we can gather, the Chancellor has come back from
France with what he wanted. That's one cause for smiling.
When you think of the state of grievance the French have been
in, ever since you divorced their King and rode off with your own
property—that's a second cause for smiling. *Où se sont évanouis
le Poitou et l'Aquitaine?*

ELEANOR. Marshal, you've gone out of your mind.

MARSHAL. You must admit, ma'am, that was a pretty damned
effective joke. When you think of them seeing the Kingdom of
France reduced by a half, on one Palm Sunday afternoon.

ELEANOR. You expect me to believe that this grin on your face has
been there for eleven years? Now tell me the truth. What is the
joke? Are the filthy actors out in the yard?

MARSHAL. No, ma'am. It's the King and the Chancellor.

ELEANOR. Being witty enough to make all men smile. Or was it
horse-play?

[9]

MARSHAL. Both, ma'am.

ELEANOR. This island can never have been better entertained.

MARSHAL. There they were, the King and the Chancellor,
Riding together along Cheapside, the crown
And the croney, in great pleasure together.
There was a fairly disgusting beggar-man,
Best part naked, lifting up one of his crutches
Across the King's path. 'Poor lousy fellow',
The King said, reining in his horse.—'Dear lord of justice',
Said the beggar. He knew his onions; he understood
Just how to come at the King's generosity.
He said he was born at Le Mans, the same as the King.
Everybody knows what affection the King has
For his own birthplace. And then a hard-up story
That jerked a quick tear out of the King. 'Christ,'
He said, 'we'll have no naked men. Christ's
Charity, Thomas, let him have your cloak!'
'Give him yours, Henry,' Becket said:
'This is *your* deed of grace.' 'It's too old, and too short',
Said the King. 'It would be no charity to his arse.'
And he made a grab at the Chancellor's cloak—cinnamon
Velvet, a new one—and they wrestled on horseback, to take it
And keep it, until every man round was laughing himself
To water, and the Chancellor gave in.
So the King threw down the cloak, obliterating
The beggar, and we all rode forward happy.

ELEANOR. A deed of grace, gracefully done,
And very delicately reported. Here is the King.

> [WILLIAM MARSHAL *withdraws. Enter* HENRY, *chuckling,*
> *and* BECKET.

HENRY. His dignity shaken, but thanks to me
There's much joy in heaven over his charity.

[10]

BECKET. Ma'am, you will have to excuse a naked Chancellor.

ELEANOR. As God made you, Becket. I've no objection.

HENRY. Embrace him, Eleanor. He has worked his charms
  On Paris.

ELEANOR. I heard so. It's a happy thing
  That he lives in this modern world, to give us his company.

BECKET. There would be no Becket, without the King.
  Nor, I might add, much sign of the King's magnificence
  Without his Chancellor. I shall be ruined, Henry,
  Trying to keep up your personal splendour for you,
  To match the importance of your position!

HENRY.   You love it.

BECKET. It's just as well I love it. It impressed Louis.

ELEANOR. Poor Louis with his endless daughters.
  It would rather seem, if he is letting us marry
  Our young Henry to the baby Margaret,
  He despairs at last of having a son. The skies
  Are curiously empty for Louis, his long prayers
  Are ineffectual.

BECKET.   Completely so.
  And his disappointed Majesty of France
  Has come to an agreement with us over the question
  Of his daughter's dowry. He is willing—at least,
  I'll say he is prepared, when the children marry
  To make over to his daughter the country of the Vexin.

ELEANOR. With all its castles. Of course, Becket.
  It was what you went for.

HENRY.   So you can chew
  On that, Becket. No commendation from Eleanor.
  She learned her behaviour from an oracle;

[11]

What she expects, is what occurs. And what
You went for, we have got. And what we have got
Is natural, because it was necessary.
And that puts us clearly into the ascendent
For a term of good order, while we do our work.
From the Arctic circle to the Pyrenees
The King's peace is holding secure.

BECKET. And God's peace, too, no doubt.

HENRY.   No doubt.
It wouldn't surprise me.
Not a son is born to Louis, though he would give
God his place in his bed if he could get one.
But four good boys to me.
There's God articulate, if ever a god spoke.
Four strong Plantagenet males born
To a kingdom worthy of God's admiration.

ELEANOR. All being well.

HENRY.   What isn't well already
Is getting down on to its knees to be cured.
God's light, there's no anarchy to come worse
Than I've already transformed into good government,
Unless they drive me to a harrowing of hell.

ELEANOR. Or unless you drive them back to anarchy
To be free of your endless tramping up and down.
I never see a man in the Court who hasn't a limp,
The soles of his feet as raw with blisters
As yours are, Henry. For the Queen's peace,
Will you sit down?

HENRY. Why not? I should like to know if there's anything
Our dear friend here of the ten talents
Can fail at. Put him in command of the field,

[12]

You can see the horse under him grow two hands taller
While Becket stacks the countryside with Christian
Corpses. Eh, Tom? And has to be restrained.
Ship him to the continent as Chancellor
To work a delicate diplomacy,
He treats the road to Paris to such an immense
Procession of the mad world, and all singing in dialect:
Hawks, and dogs; and longtailed apes
Up on the backs of the horses: all his gold plate
And his private chapel, a holy menagerie
Of opulence and power—
Every mouth in France drops too wide open
To shut again in time to deny us
Anything we came to ask.
But then you see him here, dispensing charity,
There's the deacon in him. What are you, Becket?
Force, craft, or the holy apprentice?

BECKET. The King's representative. And full of faults.
I do what I can.

HENRY. But you're not the whole of a man's capability,
Thomas, for all your talents: I know you to be
An incorruptible virgin: your virginity's
As crass extravagant as the rest of your ways of living.
If every man gave up women in God's name,
Where in God's name would be the men
To give up women in a generation's time?
I tell you, Becket, for the sake of divine worship
You'd better apply the flesh.

BECKET.   I am content,
Henry, to be one man, and not the human race.

ELEANOR. It's as well that there should be someone in this country
To undertake chastity for the King.

HENRY [*a pause*]. Well, there you have your permission.
Fill the office of my virginity
And scrape a living out of it if you can.

BECKET. Perfectly willing.

HENRY.   I shall expect a sainthood
When my term of the world is over. Put it to the Pope.
                    [*He has shuffled over some documents.*
Have you seen this, Becket? These crozier-clutching monkeys,
Ramming home their shutters against the common
Light of day: but the day comes, despite 'em!

BECKET. What is it?

HENRY [*throwing a parchment at him*]. There it is.

ELEANOR. Clearly the findings of an ecclesiastical court.

BECKET [*reading*]. The case of the Canon of Lincoln.

HENRY. The reverend Canon of rape and murder, who thinks
Because they shaved his head in a holy circle
He can grow the hair of an ape on his breast and his genitals.
He thinks he has the divine right
To cut throats and not hang for it.

BECKET.   The Bishop
Could find no proof of his guilt. That was why he was acquitted.

HENRY. They can reverse the acquittal. The Sheriff
Has sworn the man is guilty. They can pass him over
To the secular arm, where a man is known by his crimes
And not by his credentials. God's seat,
I mean to make a fair and governable England;
One justice, not two. The Church will soon
Turn every criminal into a priest, to avoid the gallows;
And the other honest, poor damned sons of Cain
Who get slewed into crime in a five-minute passion
Are hanged by the neck.

[14]

BECKET. All right, Henry.
Let's leave the poor damned sons of Cain to God, then.

ELEANOR. At least for this afternoon. We met here
To welcome Becket. As I am neither a Bishop
Nor a raping Canon
It's no argument which need detain me.

HENRY. I've heard no argument. Tom loves the law,
And he knows as well as I do the day is soon coming
When those who deviate will be compelled
Into the common pattern. There it is:
Patience restored. Sit down. I'll tell you
What my memory is celebrating today.
Not only Becket's triumphant return.
What else makes this a feast of the Angevin succession?

ELEANOR. What day is it?

HENRY. Unhorsed at the first shock.

ELEANOR. What day of the month?

BECKET. The sixteenth of September.
I can think of nothing: no battle, no marriage, no birth,
No death, no treaty, of which the anniversary
Falls on the sixteenth of September.

ELEANOR. I remember
Very well. It was the day, eleven years ago,
When I first met him; or, to be accurate,
The day I suffered his invasion:
For I can tell you, Becket,
He came forward to kiss my hand
Like a man who has just broken down the door.
I'm not at all certain he didn't ride in
Through the doorway on a horse.

[15]

HENRY. Becket, I swear
I sidled in like an egg-bound goose,
I held her in such tremendous awe, this woman
Who had been the inspiration of poets
Ever since I could understand language,
And the haunter of male imagination
Ever since I could understand sex.

ELEANOR. You hear him
Working at his arithmetic, Becket,
And grubbing up his advantage of years.

BECKET. Time walks by your side, ma'am, unwilling to pass.
But Henry lives and does his work
In a race of nights and days which are piling the years
Up on him fast.

HENRY. Twenty-nine, you methusalem!
I can live to bury you twice over. God knows
Time isn't a fellow workman to be trusted
In any great patient endeavour. It's never
Far from my mind. So much the more
The men who impede me had better take care.

ELEANOR. We were beginning to tame him. Now he's off
Trying to walk time to a standstill. Come back to the past,
Henry—eleven years ago today—

HENRY. By God, I went to her cap in hand,
Heart in mouth, and by God she was everything
Reported of her.

BECKET. And more, Henry.

ELEANOR. No, no;
I protest at that. Less, as God will judge me,
I was less than reported. My reputation
Wasn't spared in the French court then. And, to cap all,

As a variation of boredom, I gave to Louis
Another disastrous daughter. A waste of labour.
And the Abbot of Clairvaux—
After praying, I hope, for the accurate word—
Called me the evil genius of France.
That was at least something to be
In that miserable autumn, but not
My entire ambition. And, more or less then,
The door was torn off its hinges by the Duke of Normandy.
Henry was standing there eyeing me, ready
To start creating the world.

HENRY.   And not by accident,
    This meeting with her. It was in the great
    Pattern of events. Old Merlin predicted it.

BECKET. Stuff and nonsense.

HENRY.   That's your opinion.

BECKET. Well, I can think of better springs of action
    Than a popular forgery.

HENRY.   Not the cause: I never said so:
    But a welcome confirmation.

ELEANOR. You see how easily a woman is fooled, Becket.
    In the tender fancy of my heart I thought
    He was marrying me for my great possessions.
    But you see I was only a superstition.
    He took me, as he would take the salt he spilled,
    And threw me over his shoulder to improve his luck.

HENRY. The Queen is angling for a quarrel, Becket,
    Because she knows she is looking as ageless
    As the Sea of Marmara, and no one has said so.

BECKET. I have said so.

HENRY.   Then say it again;
  She likes to hear you.

ELEANOR.   Being the wife of Louis
  Was like being married to a priest; with Henry
  It is like being married to a jobbing Jupiter.
  Tell me, how was Louis when you saw him, Becket?

BECKET. Courteous, ma'am, and over anxious.

ELEANOR. Unchanged. Frayed to ribbons whether to be
  A king or an archbishop. It was always so.
  He could never co-ordinate the two worlds.

BECKET. It was charming to see him
  Pressing back against the wall at the sight
  Of the least little monk, to let him take precedence,
  Though the little monk drowned himself in blushes
  And would have given his life
  To have been allowed to bow himself out backwards.
  But the King went on murmuring, 'No, no, dear and beloved
  Brother in Christ Jesus, after you, if you please;
  My kingdom is nothing to the kingdom of heaven;
  You have the superiority; I must insist!'

HENRY. Excellent, I can hear him! You're any man
  You want to be, Becket, I told you! Let's hear him again!

ELEANOR. As in Passion week eleven years ago.

HENRY. Louis, divorce your wife; excuse me,
  I have a use for her.

ELEANOR.   Your evil spirit
  Is prepared to leave you, Louis.

BECKET [in the voice of Louis].   Then may heaven
  Help me with grace to suffer your going,
  Amen; and France, taking the lower place,

Be first in God's mercy, and bear all things patiently
In the service of heaven.

HENRY.   Amen, amen.

ELEANOR.   Am I free, Louis?

BECKET [*in the voice of Louis*].
If to St. Peter's chair and in the will of God
We are not one, by my obedience we are two.

ELEANOR. Redemption by divine arithmetic!
[*They break into laughter.*

HENRY. Which reminds me, Tom: I'm giving you Canterbury.
By your own merit, Archbishop as well as Chancellor.
[*A silence.* BECKET *stands frozen.*

HENRY. Well, you immeasurable man. Your air
Of astonished innocence doesn't convince me. Don't
Pretend you never considered the chance of this
In one of your forward-looking silences
As soon as you knew that Theobald was dead?

BECKET. This is what Louis tried to do:
Insisting on his Chancellor for a bishopric
Against the nomination of the Chapter.
And you know what came of it. The Pope intervened
With anathema, and Louis had to give in.

HENRY. Louis can only get daughters, and I get sons,
Even on the same wife. What's the argument?

BECKET. There's one man in particular, Foliot of London,
And six or seven others besides, who by
Their learning, integrity, piety, loyalty
And cast of mind, are a better choice for Canterbury.

HENRY. And who is a better choice for England?

[19]

BECKET. Any mere minor canon or choirmaster
　　Living as intently to his church
　　As a workman who bows his head
　　Over his chosen craft.

HENRY.　　　　　　　And who
　　Is a better choice for me?

BECKET.　　　　　　　I am not.
　　Ask any hundred random men,
　　They'll tell you so. The Church itself
　　Neither waits for me, nor wants me; rather
　　Deplores me than otherwise. And I'm not a man
　　Whose confidence thrives on its own. What I do well
　　I do because men believe I will do it well
　　Before ever the thing is begun. The fruit
　　On the tree forms larger in a willing climate,
　　Or anyway I found it so in my own
　　Experience. I care for men's opinion.
　　I doubt if I should ever be
　　Sufficient in myself, to hold my course
　　Without any approval. No one would say
　　I was made of the stuff of martyrs. So if you ever
　　Trusted to my perception—

HENRY.　　　　　　　Never,
　　My friend. I trust your administration,
　　Grasp of the law, charm of persuasion,
　　And your like-thinking with my own thought—

BECKET. Natural in a Chancellor.

HENRY.　　　　　　　And natural
　　In my long-tried friend, Tom Becket.

BECKET. But what is natural in an Archbishop?

HENRY. Precisely what is natural in Tom Becket.
    Your election is simple. To the majority
    Of men, inevitable.

BECKET.   One thing is simple.
    Whoever is made Archbishop will very soon
    Offend either you, Henry, or his God.
    I'll tell you why. There is a true and living
    Dialectic between the Church and the state
    Which has to be argued for ever in good part.
    It can't be broken off or turned
    Into a clear issue to be lost or won.
    It's the nature of man that argues;
    The deep roots of disputation
    Which dug in the dust, and formed Adam's body.
    So it's very unlikely, because your friend
    Becomes Primate of England, the argument will end.
    As Chancellor, my whole mind could speak for yours,
    Because I knew the Church had for her tongue
    A scholar and a saintly man who was not to be
    Brow-beaten. But now Theobald is dead.
    The English Church has lost its tongue. Do you mean
    That I should now become that tongue,
    To be used in argument between you and me?
    Because, if so, we shall not be as we have been.

HENRY. You will miss your falcons, of course, if you decide
    That blood sports are too secular.
    But which of us is going to change his nature
    Or his understanding? Together we have understood
    The claims men have on us
    And how to meet them. Whatever your office
    This truth is unalterable, the truth being one.

BECKET. The truth, like all of us, being of many dimensions,

C

And men so placed, they stake their lives on the shape of it
Until by a shift of their position, the shape
Of truth has changed.

ELEANOR.   Hardly a conclusion, I fancy,
Which the good scholar and saintly man who trained you
Would have applauded with both hands. Nevertheless
Consider it, Henry. Conserve the blessings
You have already.

HENRY.   The blessings I have already
Are there to be blessed with.
And the future is waiting to be blessed by us,
In spite of the men who drag their feet. I can see
He means to refuse.

BECKET.   I haven't said so.

HENRY. I can see he means to.

BECKET.   I haven't said so.
But listen to the things I fear. However much
We both imperatively want it otherwise,
You're dividing us, and, what is more, forcing
Yourself and me, indeed the whole kingdom,
Into a kind of intrusion on the human mystery,
Where we may not know what it is we're doing,
What powers we are serving, or what is being made of us.
Or even understand the conclusion when it comes.
Delivering us up, in fact, to universal workings
Which neither you nor I wish to comply with
Or even to contemplate. If this should be so,
Do you still propose that I should accept Canterbury?

ELEANOR. Well, which is it to be, Henry, to predict
The future, Becket or Merlin?

HENRY.   Now he's master of excuses.
  Too complacent, is he, to enlarge himself
  To the size of the new world we have under our hand?
  But foresee this, then: if King and Archbishop
  Can work in affection, the Church will be content
  And calm. If not: waste of hours, energy,
  Opportunity; and much loss
  And peril to souls will come of it; and, worse,
  Loss of the time we need, to give England
  An incorruptible scaffolding of law
  To last her longer than her cliffs.

BECKET.   You remember
  When the Archbishop was dying, he sent for me
  And I didn't go. Now, on your own insistence,
  I see I do go after all, though now
  Too late to have any happiness in going.
  According to your will, then, Henry.

HENRY. All right, you confer the favour. I thought that I did.
  But what difference? We shall go ahead.
  Make away with your uncertainties, man.
  Anything unaccustomed has a doubtful look
 ·Till it grows to be a part of our thinking.
  Why shouldn't you keep your falcons?
  God will expect something of the kind
  From an Archbishop who was born in England.
  We'll make up to Him for it by establishing
  Order, protection, and justice
  For the man who has a shirt or the man who has not.
  A pity the whole of the earth is not to be
  Serene in our keeping. But there are still
  The four good Plantagenet males to come.
  We must leave them something to do.

[23]

Come and see that nest of young eagles, Tom.
You can describe to Harry the good points
Of Margaret of France, if you think you can make
An infant sound like a desirable wife.

ELEANOR. You've drawn blood from Becket, Henry.
The city sunshine, and the new English archbishop
Are equally cold and pale.
And besides, he has made a long journey for you.
You should give him time to rest.

BECKET.   The sea was rough.

HENRY. Do as you like, Tom. Be your own man
Until tomorrow.   [*Exit* HENRY.

ELEANOR.   And, ever after, be his
In every particular. The free and fallen
Spirits we may think we are,
You and I and the nest of young eagles,
Have our future state only in a world of Henry.
I should go and get your rest, Becket, before
You are led away into captivity by this new well-ordered world.
          [*She follows* HENRY. BECKET *stands unmoving.* WILLIAM
          MARSHAL *comes forward with a cloak.*

MARSHAL. They've brought over another cloak for you from the
Chancery, my lord Chancellor.—Will you wear it, my lord?—
They brought it to replace the one you parted with.—This is
your own, from the Chancery, sir.
          [*He puts the cloak on to* BECKET'*s shoulders.*

BECKET. Is the day much colder?

MARSHAL. I don't think so. But, if you remember, you gave away
your cloak—

BECKET. Tell me, Marshal, do you know yourself, who you are?

[24]

MARSHAL. I daresay I could pick myself out among two or three men, if I took thought.

BECKET. You have the best of it.—Take good care of the King.

MARSHAL. Why not? And the King can take good care of us. But what's your thought there, sir?

[BECKET *moves on out of sight.*

Why urge that on me?—[*He turns to the audience.*] I was soon to know. What was one had become two. The simple and reasonable action, at the very moment it came to life, was neither simple nor limited to reason. There it is. The logic of events has never been argued in the schools, as far as I know. There was the morning full of life, like an unbroken colt; but the moment the King, with a good will and strong knees, got astride it, God only knows what whistle it was answering; but it made history, whatever that is.— The day when Becket was consecrated Archbishop was a bright, fresh day; what clouds there were were easy-moving; and, except for a sharp indrawing of breath from the Chapter at Canterbury, we were all in the humour of progress, the rich men inside the cathedral, wary over their privileges, or the poor men outside, concerned with hope, all for the moment willing to presume a benefit from this move the King had made: firm, reasonable, new for those who looked for change, not too new for those who prospered in stability, and therefore promising, making for unity. The whole significance of unity was not debated, nor what fires can forge a diverse multitude into one mind. But for the present, at any rate. . . . Excuse me. [*He peers into the shadows.*] Come here.

[BLAE *comes forward.*

Who let you through?

BLAE. Nobody let me through. He was dead against it. I didn't need any youngster like that to tell me to stand and be recognized. I know who I am as well as he does. What I've come for is no business of his.

MARSHAL. This is no such free world, sweetheart. Come on, I'll see you safely outside again.

BLAE. I wouldn't put you to the trouble.—Keep your hands for your food.

MARSHAL. The boys all know where to find you, don't worry. If business is so bad, coming here isn't going to change it.

BLAE. Change isn't what I came for. I want something taken care of.

MARSHAL. I'll take care of you, for a good start. You can follow the Court when it's out on the road, but when we are back to London you stay home.

BLAE. So I do. But there's something I have to say to the King.

MARSHAL. You're not going to see the King.

BLAE. I don't have to; I can tell who he is in the dark.

MARSHAL. So that's what you're up to. Then let me say this to you, if you haven't got sense enough to know it; there's a private world, and a public world, there's a world of night, and a world of day, and if you dare to get one confused with the other I'll break my heart for the way you'll end up. The sooner I get you out of here, the better it will be for you.

BLAE. The King will see no harm comes to me, I can tell you that now.

MARSHAL. The King isn't going to have the chance.
                              [*He throws her over his shoulder.*

BLAE. He won't have you do this, not to the mother of a son of his.
                    [MARSHAL *stops and puts her down.* HENRY *stands upstage, unseen by them.*

MARSHAL. That's a pretty presentable story. Born with a label tied to his ear, *filius Henrici*, with a birth-mark of the Plantagenet leopard stamped sheer across him.

[26]

BLAE. You might have seen him. How did you know?

MARSHAL. Because otherwise you'd be out of your mind to risk laying charges against the King for the sake of what you can get out of it. I can tell you now what you'll get out of it—

HENRY. How do you know he's a boy of mine?

BLAE. It's him!

MARSHAL [*aside to her*]. Now will you run?

BLAE [*under her breath*]. I'm not doing wrong.

HENRY. How do you know he's a boy of mine?

BLAE. He says it himself, sir, in every pug look he gives me.

HENRY. What do you want?

BLAE. To know what's to be done with him. That's all, sir. What's to be done with you, I say to him, playing about with half the muck of your father's kingdom on your face and your knees?

HENRY. Go and take a look at him, Marshal. If he looks like mine, bring him to me. If he looks like mine to me, Becket can raise him and train him at the Chancery.

BLAE. Sir, you're a good King, a good man to all of us.

HENRY. Go and lick him clean, and give my face a chance to shine through him. And don't expect anything more from it.

BLAE. Nothing on earth, you can have my word. Myself is myself, sir, and that I can make do to look after. I give you my word—

HENRY. All right; exist unexplained. Get home.

BLAE. Yes, sir, my lord. [*Exit* BLAE.

HENRY. You see what comes, Marshal, of a wet summer.
That August at Hereford, the rain came down on us
Like a high sea slapping over a cockle boat

For six days, remember?
A week of good life wasted in a flood.

[*A* CLERIC *has entered with a letter.*
What's this?

CLERIC.　　　　From his Grace of Canterbury, my lord.
He sends you his love and obedience.

HENRY. Two words, love and obedience. What
Does he expect me to do with them, when I never see him?
Haven't I given him time enough yet
To get used to being cock of the cloistral walk?
There's a child in him; he loves himself
In a new frock. That's it, Marshal, you fetch
That sprig of Plantagenet the whore has got,
And we'll make him as good a Chancellor in twenty years.
We'll see what life comes out of that churn-up
Of rain and Hereford mud and boredom and semen
And prostitution. Go and fetch him.

MARSHAL. I'll take a look, my lord, and try and judge what I find
there.

[*Exit* MARSHAL. HENRY, *who has broken open the letter, reads it.*

HENRY. Did he tell you to say his love and obedience?

CLERIC. Yes, my lord.

HENRY. Then he told you a lie.

CLERIC. My lord?

HENRY. He made you bring me a damned lie! Watch out, you pious
little fellow, how much of your heart you give to faith. We've
hanged God once, to fulfil the scriptures. So now tell me what
reason God still has to keep the strain of treachery so active in us.
Eh? You tell me that.

CLERIC. Oh, my lord, watch your words.

HENRY. What kind of a farce is good faith and loyalty?

ELEANOR [*standing upstage*]. You tell me that.

HENRY [*looking at her*]. I am hurt by the child in this Tom Becket.
[*Enter* GILBERT FOLIOT, *Bishop of London, the King's confessor.*

ELEANOR. What has he done?

HENRY. Resigned from the Chancellorship, with his love and
obedience. Come here, Foliot. You'd better absolve me of a
blasphemy, or something of the sort. It upset our holy innocent,
here.

FOLIOT. Are you truly penitent?

HENRY. Yes, yes, yes, come on!
[FOLIOT *begins to speak in Latin, the words of absolution,
and then breaks off.*

FOLIOT. *Ego te absolvo*—My lord, will you give me your attention?

HENRY [*still reading Becket's letter*]. God in a suicide's grave! Will
you listen to this? . . . 'Not wishing now to be in the royal court
. . . diddle, diddle, diddle . . . to have leisure for prayers, and to
superintend the business of the Church . . .'—Who put him there
to pray? There are ten thousand monks, with nothing else to do
except say his prayers for him.
[FOLIOT *concludes the absolution, fairly hurriedly:*

FOLIOT. *—in nomine patris et filii et spiritu sancti.*

HENRY. Amen.—Christ in glory, what's been the truth of him over
these years? The whole motive and labour of his mind, as he
showed it to us, was the wise conduct of this poor, tormented
kingdom. And he made a fortune out of it, which I didn't grudge
him. But, by God, that was all he cared for, to be the unsurpass-
able Becket, and nothing at all for the shaping of a just world: his
mouth was making words at me, like a purse farting.

[29]

ELEANOR. Now he will see your justice demonstrated,
This angelic justice,
Hearing all voices, and weighing them in its heart,
Having no person or desires. Show us, Henry.

HENRY. Where is he, then? Ever since his consecration
He has turned his back on us, crouching down in Canterbury
As though he had conquered a rock, stuck his cross on it,
And meant to keep a sulking stretch of water
Between him and me.

CLERIC. Sir, speaking of what we see at Canterbury, you would
praise, as we do, how the finger of God has touched him; how
utterly he has put aside all ostentation; how he feasts the poor,
visits the sick, and every day washes the feet of thirteen beggars.

HENRY. A very sagacious and elaborate performance. I hope the
beggars are paid for it.

FOLIOT. We must remember, my lord, the difficulties for him are
very great. An immense talent, as we know; but, even so, even
you, my lord, must have expected an uncertain period of
readjustment. He is anxious to please. It will be interesting to see
how he achieves what you have set him to do.

HENRY. We know you will be interested. So does he. The devil of
an interest.

FOLIOT. False. I had no ambition to be in his place, though I
believe it was said.

HENRY. It was said so, I believe. But you deny it. Love and
obedience have been said. But here it's denied. When do we have
the truth?

Enter BECKET

ELEANOR. Ask him.   [HENRY *turns his head away.*
He has left his rock.

HENRY. What am I supposed to make of this?

BECKET. What is natural because it is necessary.
    I am one man, not two. My heart and reason
    Both give me the same answer.

HENRY.   I can see no heart.
    What reason?

BECKET.   You gave me spiritual charge of the kingdom.
    I take it, then, the kingdom's need
    Is that I should carry this charge in good earnest.

HENRY. The kingdom, not a country parish. You know
    Very well the need of the kingdom you serve.
    It's a living land, not a charge of kneeling peasants
    Obedient to a bell. And you know the Church
    That you're the head of, with its delight in substance
    Growing on itself like sin. Power and privilege,
    The swollen spiritual legs we have to stand on!
    I'll tell you, Becket, why it is you have drained
    All the warmth out of yourself down there in Canterbury.
    Because the King's truth is the truth you still believe.
    You kept clear of me to give yourself
    A spiritual authority you know you're weak in.
    What's your answer to that?

BECKET.   If it is true
    That I'm weak in spiritual authority—it isn't
    For me to deny it—should you not thank God
    That I mean to gain it? What is the worth of a kingdom
    If the head of its Church has no spiritual authority?

HENRY. What is the worth of spiritual authority
    If the lives under it are lived in anarchy?

BECKET. What have I done that proposes anarchy?

HENRY. Contradictory power is what you propose.
There is hardly one thing I have reached out for
In these last months, which hasn't been obstructed
From Canterbury. But I see you, Becket:
You mean the Church to be answerable for nothing
Except itself, and yourself to be answerable
Only to the old would-be infallible Italian
Who rattles his keys of heaven and hell whichever
Way expedience turns him.

FOLIOT.   *Te absolvo.* My lord,
Whatever the provocation, there's no advantage
In turning your scorn on the Holy Father.

HENRY. Is there not? Then I'm taking no advantage.

BECKET. Henry, one of us there has to be
To whom the single care is not of this world.

HENRY. Very well; give up this world.
Contend against me like an opposite.
See that the spiritual power is powerful in the spirit.
Indeed, go on, be smitten with a great light
And relieve us all of a load of darkness.
Show us, my friend—we are hungry to see it—
The humility, the patience, and the poverty,
The movement into grace, the entire surrender
And sacrifice of the self.
And not by a demonstration of foot-washing.

BECKET. Why suddenly talk like a woman,
Contriving an argument when you know the answers?
You, Henry, of all men, who cry out
For a demonstration of order, for a house of men
So lucid and strong it will never be confounded.
See the Church likewise. If she should have

[32]

No definition in terms of the world, no shepherd
To guard her rule and substance, she would soon be thrust
Into any corner that man, trampling forward
Towards his places of possession,
Thought fit to leave open. What is not seen or heard
But yet endures has to be shown and spoken.
How, then, without rich form of ritual
And ceremony, shall we convey
The majesty of eternal government,
Or give a shape to the mystery revealed
Yet as a mystery?

HENRY. All right, perform the mystery, demonstrate
The mysterious order: baptize us, reprove us,
Absolve us, and bury us; but in so far
As your body sweats like the rest of us,
You owe me obedience.

BECKET.   And in so far
As you live, Henry, like the rest of us
In a universe of powers outside your government:
And in so far
As everything beyond the immediate moment
Ends in speculation: and in so far
As not even the predictions of Merlin
Can provide us with a living geometry
Of what we do, or what's done to us, in these
Things you owe your obedience to the Church.

HENRY. I owe no obedience to a man who cheats my trust in him.
None at all to an ostentatious humbug
Who dragged himself up by the shoulders of the kingdom
And once up, kicked it away. Your breeding
Wasn't prepared for the full extent of your talents,
Not to serve this world, or God either.

BECKET. You have borne with me pretty well. I must live in hope
That God's patience won't fall far short of yours, my lord.
—Your permission to withdraw.

HENRY.   In a fury, good;
You're still living, then; there's a warmth
Residing somewhere in this reverend cadaver.

BECKET. I will go apart for a time.

HENRY.   Do, for a time,
And scour yourself with an hour of good thinking.
Return Tom Becket, a man unwilling to deceive
Either himself or me.

> [BECKET *turns as though to speak again.* FOLIOT *touches his arm.*

FOLIOT. Apart, apart. You are not ready to speak. This need never
have happened. Come away.

> [BECKET *moves away,* FOLIOT *and the* CLERIC *with him.*
> HENRY *turns aside to* WILLIAM MARSHAL, *who has returned.*

HENRY. Well, what's the answer?

MARSHAL. I saw the boy. He struck at me with a fist the size of
an acorn and told me I was an old what I am not, my lord.

HENRY. Would you say he is mine?

MARSHAL. Dead sure he is.

HENRY. Did you fetch him away?

MARSHAL. Yes, I did; I brought him back in my arms, and had
my guts nearly kicked into my back. It's a painful commission,
bringing home the future. Do you want to see him, sir, before
I take him to the Chancery?

HENRY. When he's Chancellor he can go to the Chancery.

MARSHAL. But how's this, my lord? I thought you said—

[34]

HENRY. You can go to the Chancery; you can fetch young Henry out of Becket's care, and his little wife with him.

MARSHAL. He was shaping well. Why move him?

HENRY. There's a change in the spirit of the Chancery.

MARSHAL. The boy loves the Chancellor—the Archbishop; spiritual shepherd and uncle-schoolmaster. I doubt if he'll leave the Chancery without tears. And I'm already thoroughly drenched and salted from the first one.

HENRY. We have seen the remarkable steady mind of self-love. We've nothing further to learn of that, Marshal. Fetch the boy home, and keep him in your own charge. Teach him good faith.

MARSHAL. I? Teach him?

HENRY. Good faith.

MARSHAL. I'm no schoolmaster.

HENRY. Well, then, be the book. Leave him alone to study from you.

MARSHAL [*turning to go*]. As you say.

HENRY [*his voice rising in pain*].
Tell me how a man who has seen eye to eye with me
Can suddenly look at me as if he was blind?

MARSHAL [*turning back*]. Sir?

HENRY.   Fetch the boy home.
[MARSHAL *pauses for a moment as though to speak, then goes gravely away.* HENRY *slowly turns and faces the place where* BECKET *stood, as though squaring up for a fight.*

HENRY. Now . . . Becket.

CURTAIN

END OF ACT ONE

[35]

ACT TWO

ELEANOR

BECKET

HENRY

GILBERT FOLIOT

WILLIAM MARSHAL

EARL OF LEICESTER

BLAE

YOUNG HENRY, *the King's son*

RICHARD

GEOFFREY } *his brothers*

JOHN

ROGER, *Blae's son*

MESSENGER

BECKET'S CROSS-BEARER

BISHOPS AND MEN OF THE COURT

ACT TWO · 1163-70

BECKET, *with the* BISHOPS. *Enter* ELEANOR.

ELEANOR. I can hardly wish you Goodmorning, Archbishop,
When the morning is so unwilling to appear.
> [*She bows to them, as they bow to her.*
My lords. Could you see your way across the yard?

BECKET. By groping, ma'am.

ELEANOR.   Have you come to find the King?
Today's a poor day for finding any man;
Only sounds and voices, and half creations of the fog
Which move like men but fade like spirits.

BECKET. It's a murk which penetrates the flesh
And wraps round the bones. No day for the mind.

ELEANOR. Or the light foot. It's a hard, subtle terrain
You have come to cross in Henry, Becket.
Please heaven some good comes out of it.
For me (a woman who dreads an abstract passion)
It presents a chilling prospect. These London streets,
Which I seem to have to walk as a penance
For loving life too warmly, tolerate me
Less every day. And you have lost
Your genius for life, that ready sense of the world
Which used to give your gravity a charm
And your laughter a solemnity,
As though you sang the complex heart of reality
And by singing mastered it. How could worship
Or prayer do better?

BECKET.   Alas, madam.

ELEANOR.   Alas,
  Becket!

BECKET.   God must guide me.

ELEANOR.   To guide the God
  A little is sometimes not without merit. But I see
  The only way I can have any part in life
  Is to stand and be the curious onlooker
  While two unproved worlds fly at each other.
  Be sure you draw blood, to lift my drooping spirits.
  The ground under your feet
  Has become the sand of the arena.
  And here's the bull you are matched with.
        [ELEANOR *moves away as* HENRY *enters, with* COURTIERS.

HENRY.   You had better throw some light on this new man
  The Archbishop, Archbishop. We're losing precious weeks.
  Every day men are born into an island
  Not yet ready to receive them.
  I need reassurance.

BECKET.   Of what, reassurance of what?
  Whether indeed there can ever be a world
  Answering to the man created?

HENRY.   To achieve
  That is our whole concern. Suppose you tell me
  How you see your own part in the process.

BECKET.   To protect us from going aground on deceptive time,
  To keep our course in the deep reality.
  As time is contained in eternity
  So is temporal action contained in eternal truth.
  And that truth can't be put at the mercy of time.

HENRY. Nor time at the mercy of an ambitious Church.
I will remind you of what you know already.
There are certain customs,
Part of the growing nature of this island,
Which many generations in their need and experience
Have made their own in a common law. And these,
For what better will come of them, we mean to maintain.
You're well aware of them:
Clerics, for a crime against the common law,
To answer to the King's court.

BECKET.   No doubt
You have noticed, by my wish the bishops' courts
Have made their judgements more severe.

HENRY. Very tactful and unimpressive. There have been
Already in my time a hundred murders
Which were settled by nothing but a futile fine
Or the lick of a prison.

BECKET.   There would have been two hundred
If we had hanged the murderers. As it is,
There are now a hundred men who see we think
Lives of more account than they did: spirits
In trust, which we must never despair of.

HENRY. Men who make a profession of God should expect
The heavier punishment.

BECKET.   They are still men.

HENRY. Indeed they are! Therefore we need to know
Who is to govern them. Let me go on.
Laymen brought up for trial before a bishop
Must be given in every instance legal witnesses.
No archbishop, bishop, or beneficed clerk
To leave the kingdom without my authority.

No one holding land of me, nor any
Minister of mine to be excommunicated
Without my knowledge. For this is what you do,
You lords of the Church Arrogant,
Like an old god crazy with his thunderbolts.
As for the rest of the problems hindering our hope,
You know them closely, having shared them.
But that was then, when I knew you. As things are,
I need your word that you'll obey these Customs.

BECKET. God said 'I am Truth', not 'I am Custom'.

HENRY. Whose truth are you, you acrobat? These Customs
Are the truth of the men whose lives shaped them.

BECKET. What a man knows he has by experience,
But what a man is precedes experience.
His experience merely reveals him, or destroys him;
Either drives him to his own negation,
Or persuades him to his affirmation, as he chooses.
And this truth is not custom.
This is not under the law, but under grace.
What you see as the freedom of the State
Within the law, I fear, as the enslavement
Of that other state of man, in which, and in
Which only, he can know his perfect freedom.
So this is how I must answer you:
We obey you in everything, unless it should threaten
The will of God, and the laws and dignity of the Church.

HENRY. 'Unless' is nothing, no answer, and no vow!
Who is to set the limit on your laws and dignity?
Who, apart from your own reading of God,
Is going to control your ambition? Very astute,
Isn't it, to attach yourself to a power
Which proceeds and communicates only through you.

[40]

BECKET. If by me you mean the Church, tell me
   Who controls the ambitions of the State?

HENRY. The well-being of the whole community.
   What man here will undertake
   To define the will of God? We have seen it
   Mauling humanity with visitations
   Of horror beyond belief.
   If you're so devoted to this will
   Why don't you go to its aid?
   Heave your house down when the hurricane shakes it,
   Piss in the flood water. Strip those robes off, Becket,
   And stand here shuddering
   In the icy air of God's will. Or talk better sense.

BECKET. And yet here, at the mercy of these elements,
   We exist more often unharmed.
   The vehement liberty of terror, which ignores our flesh,
   Is not the will,
   But it knows the will, returns to it in calm.
   Even when in rebellion it keeps
   The signature of light. In the avalanche of snow
   The star-figure of the flake is there unchanged.
   It was out of a whirlwind that God answered Job.
   And here, too, in the whirl of our senses,
   The way for this will has to be kept unthreatened.

HENRY. The will of the people is the will of God.

BECKET. They have many wills: many lusts and many thirsts:
   A will for death as well as a will for life.
   But, quick or dormant, in th'm they have a longing
   To be worked into the eternal fabric
   By God's love. And so we go with you faithfully,
   And swear we will, only saving our order.

HENRY. Which means whatever you like to make it.
  One order is going to be saved: mine in this kingdom!
  You know as well as I do, your saving clause
  Is more effective than what you swear. You, Foliot,
  Give me a straighter answer. You, you, you, you!
  You're not so brash in your calling.

FOLIOT.   Well, my lord,
  We are here as one body. It will have to be
  As the Church is led to reply: in everything
  Obedient saving our order.

A BISHOP.   Obedient
  Saving our order.

OTHERS.   Saving our order. Our order.
                [HENRY's *anger is like an explosion of madness.*

HENRY [*with a roar*].
  Save your commonsense if you want to stay as you are!
  The Church never said this to a King before.
  By God, it's not going to begin with me!
  I had a demon for an ancestor.
  There are times I feel her wading in my blood and howling
  For a sacrifice of obscurantical fools.
  And by God, she shall have it!
  Your old immunity is over, you're trapped
  In a change of the world, my lords, which men deserve
  And are going to be given. The man who gets in the way
  Is of no more consequence than a skull
  Kicked about by oafs in a field,
  And that's what he will come to. Jesus whipped!
  You have reason to blench and hug your skirts round you,
  I'll tear the parts out of you—
  Hell doesn't have a monopoly in torment.

[42]

You will find as good here, if you pull your pious faces
When I ask for help. You'd better consider it.

> [*He leaves them in an uproar. An unnatural light begins to
> penetrate the fog. Faces are distorted by it. Shadows gesticu-
> late at a great height above the* MEN *of the Court, who rage
> against the* PRIESTS, *some advancing towards them waving
> axes. The* BISHOPS *harry* BECKET *in extreme anxiety.*

THE COURT [*the words that can be heard*].

Time it was said! They've got to learn where they live. They've
got a hold on the country beyond anything ever known. Grabbing
lands that haven't been theirs for a generation. Making us a property of Rome. [*They advance on the* BISHOPS, *some waving axes*:]
Consider, if you want to live. We'll split your heads open and
find your brains! If the road wants clearing, here's a cleaver to
do it. That's it, beat a retreat! Ah yes, now you know the times
you live in!

> [*At the same time the* BISHOPS *have moved crying out to*
> BECKET.]

BISHOPS. Have you thought where you lead us? How do we serve
the Church if we lose our Sees? Or our lives, perhaps: God
knows what he intends. You've lost us the friendship of the King.
The Holy Father said Be moderate; moderate, he said, moderate.
If you had shown a spark of your old will to please. . . . Is your
power to leave you, now you're powerful?

COURTIER. Take your time, Archbishop. The King's in dead
earnest.

BECKET. As I am.

COURT. What becomes of your influence if you rot out your life in
a dungeon, nobody even remembering where you are? And are
you so sure of your motives, with due respect, my lord? No self-
applause, no vainglory, no obstinacy? Anyway, your future, and
the Church's too, depends on the way you think.

[43]

A BISHOP. Have you thought of our distress?

BECKET [*suddenly, after silence*]. Where is the King?

ELEANOR. Ask yourself where it is you stand, saying
  Where is the King?
  Look round at the unreality of the light
  And the unreality of the faces in the light.
  You and he, you told him, would reach a place
  Where you might not know what was being made of you,
  Or understand the conclusion when it came.
  Certainly the familiar world has departed.
  A death-world here, where every move
  Is magnified on to the fog's blind face
  And becomes the gesture of a giant.

A BISHOP. You made your decision alone. Carry it alone.
      [*Enter* HENRY. *He stands in the strange light, looking at*
      BECKET. *All other eyes are also on* BECKET.

BECKET. Still with anxiety, but hoping, trusting
  That you mean to command nothing against my conscience,
  I will give you the Yes you ask for.
          [*An exhalation of relief from the* BISHOPS.

HENRY. Then we can go ahead. What do the rest say?

FOLIOT. Yes; in good faith.

BISHOPS.   In good faith. Good faith.

HENRY. You are men of admirable judgement.
  Here they are, the Customs of the kingdom,
  Codified, ready for your seal. And when it's done
  You can give us a burst of bell-ringing to clear the air.

BECKET. What's this?

HENRY. Your word made parchment. Fifteen paragraphs;
  You're familiar with all of them.

[44]

ELEANOR [*to herself*].   A false move.
  Oh, never define!

BECKET.   No! By all-prevailing
  God: no! I'll never set my seal to this.

HENRY. Ah!

BECKET [*to the* BISHOPS]. You see where being accommodating
  And afraid has brought us. Fear is the father of sin,
  The devil's best weapon is a man's nerves!

HENRY.   He agrees
  To cramming God into the words of dogma,
  But evades the simple expression of law!

BECKET [*to the* BISHOPS]. You see
  The pit that's dug for us under the spread branches.
  Dreading that I should be cast out and alone
  I was leading the Church to a broken back,
  Betraying all heaven's charge that was trusted in me:
  A poverty of spirit please God I never
  Approach again. Harder the forgiveness
  Which I now need to find. For now indeed
  I'm alone. The knowledge of my fault
  Is my only companion.   [*He moves away.*

FOLIOT [*in despair*].   Where are you leaving us?
  Fairly lying between the hammer and the anvil!

HENRY. Now you begin to know him, the bewildering
  Turns to maintain himself, first will, then won't:
  Will in the abstract, won't in the definition.
  He pretends to agree, to mask his real intentions,
  Until his bluff is called. And now we're to have
  A display of the anguished penitent
  While he looks for a way out. But I shall help him
  To bring order to this disarray of the spirit.

[45]

You reject your work as Chancellor. I'll relieve you
Of all shadow of that great and false expense.
You needn't be haunted by a sense of debt
Which might hamper your independence.
You shall pay me back every penny you received
From the estates and castles which were yours then.

BECKET [*turning*]. But you freed me from all secular obligations
The day I was consecrated.

HENRY.   Before you freed
Yourself from the purpose of the time you live in.
You will make good the sums you spent
On your war in Toulouse.

BECKET.   In the service of the State!

HENRY. It was in the service of recommending Becket
To himself and me.

BECKET.   It will somehow be paid.

HENRY [*now in full cry*].
And since the eternal account overlooks nothing,
To free your conscience by precise audit
You can pay the country back what you had from all
The vacant sees and abbeys while you were Chancellor.
Then devote yourself to God with a less hang-dog look.
    [*A moan of consternation from the* BISHOPS. BECKET *falls
    on one knee, and supports himself with a hand on the floor,
    like a pugilist waiting to rise before the end of the count.*

FOLIOT. Have you given yourself time, my lord,
To think what this means? Where will the Archbishop
Find the sureties for so much? Do you mean
To punish us all, to shake the whole spiritual power?

HENRY. Who will not be glad to share a burden
Which lightens a bowed conscience? The Archbishop

[46]

Prefers to abandon the things of this world. [*His anger returns.*]
Why should a man make God my enemy
And the enemy of a maturing nation,
As this man does? You shall see him as I found him:
A man depending on office, no nearer God
Than I am. Tell him to come back and face me.

CLERIC. Sir, he is ill, the Archbishop; he has to ask you
To excuse him; he is taken ill.

HENRY.   Contempt
Of the royal summons! He piles up his mistakes.
The more he squirms to free himself, the more
He tangles himself in guilt. Twice already
During the last month or two he has tried
To get to France without my authority,
And twice the ships have brought him back again.
It looks as if this island
Isn't large enough to contain both of us.

ELEANOR [*to herself*].
Who will grow large enough to contain the island?

HENRY. Either there are laws for every man,
And he is one; or there are no laws for any man.
The day is vital, and the world can't stand still
To be cheated, even under cover of God.

ELEANOR. Let me say this to the man who makes the world—
And also to the man who makes himself the Church.
Consider complexity, delight in difference.
Fear, for God's sake, your exact words.
Do you think you can draw lines on the living water?
Together we might make a world of progress.
Between us, by our three variants of human nature,
You and Becket and me, we could be

[47]

The complete reaching forward. Neither of you
Will dare to understand it. Have I spoken too late?

HENRY [*ignoring her*]. The issue is so great, the man so intractable,
It has come to this; he has to stand his trial,
And be judged by England, not by me,
By England's dawning knowledge of herself,
As though she tried herself in the trial of Becket.
We have done with privilege of person. None of us
Is anything more than the purpose of our time.
[*He leaves, in the diminishing light.*

ELEANOR. Who has left the most blood on the sand, Marshal?

MARSHAL. Ma'am, the Archbishop is badly gored, that's certain.
But what wounds have been made on the King we still have to
discover. This business has grown too big for me.

ELEANOR. Grown very small, Marshal: the size of two men in a
rage.
We are not going to see the great issues contending,
Nor the new spirit of England being forged in a fire.
We shall see the kicks and blows of angry men,
Both losing sight of the cause.
The high names
Of God and the State are now displaced
By hurt pride, self-distrust, foiled ambition,
And the rest of our common luggage.

MARSHAL. That may be. But, all the same, the Archbishop is on
trial.

ELEANOR. When the glorious battle turns into the vendetta
The great issues, no longer controlled by men,
Themselves take over command. Then at last he may listen
To some other voice than his own!

MARSHAL.   You mean the King?

ELEANOR. You saw, Marshal, how he turned away from me?
Am I no more distinct than the men who walk in the fog?
If I think I am a woman of flesh and blood,
And unmistakeable spirit,
He will soon undeceive me. He turned away
As he would from his shadow on the wall.

MARSHAL. But, ma'am—

ELEANOR. Go to him, Marshal: love him as you can.
He will have need of that.   [*Exit* ELEANOR.
> [*When the light returns,* FOLIOT *and another* BISHOP *are standing at one side. Enter* BECKET *with his cross-bearer* ALEXANDER LLEWELYN. *He takes the cross from* LLEWELYN.

FOLIOT. Look at this. Does he know what he's doing? [*To* BECKET.] You're ill advised, aren't you, Archbishop, to come here carrying your own cross? It's like drawing a sword out of the scabbard in the King's face. Suppose he should draw his own sword in reply? We should see a country at war with itself.

BECKET. We should know a man at war with himself. That's a risk we have to commit to God.
> [*He goes forward, using the cross as a staff in his left hand, as the* EARL OF LEICESTER *enters. He stops short as he sees* BECKET *advancing to take his seat.* BECKET *sits.*

FOLIOT [*to the* BISHOP].
A fool he was, and a fool he always will be.

BECKET [*to* LEICESTER].
What do you have to say to me? What is it?

LEICESTER. The verdict of the trial.

BECKET.   Such you call it.

LEICESTER. My lord, time has never seen before

Such a council as this, representing a whole nation
Sitting with the King in a conclave of law;
The evidence argued and weighed with deep anxiety.
And this new coherence of justice finds you
A perjurer and the King's traitor.

BECKET. Have you surrendered your mind so completely
That you can believe in this use of law?
Judgement is a sentence given after trial.
I was brought here on a pretext, not a charge.
So, for all your threshing of documents, the King
Thumbing his way through the always altering Customs,
Sweating for precedents and legal justification,
There has been no trial. And no trial can have no sentence.

LEICESTER. All you possess you hold from the King.

BECKET. Nothing. Nothing from the King. Whatever the Church
Holds is held in perpetual liberty.
I am your father, though you hold me in disdain:
Still and always your father, however vexed in thought,
Fallible in action, unpersuading in word,
Falling short in everything that makes
A man convince his times with truth. In spite
Of all, your father; and by a father's authority
I forbid you to give sentence.

LEICESTER.   Do I take
This answer to the King?

BECKET.   There is nothing
To be answered. I leave here as I came.
> [BECKET *moves away, bearing the cross, in a storm of threats
> and mocks from those of the* COURT *who are present. As*
> LEICESTER *turns to go, enter* HENRY.

HENRY. Where has he gone?

[50]

LEICESTER. He goes as he came, he said,
Refusing sentence, denying any trial.

HENRY. Fetch him back. We haven't done with him yet.

MARSHAL [*coming forward*].
This isn't the time to pursue him.
Three-quarters of the town followed him here,
And those who could, got down on their knees
And kissed the step he came in by. Take a look.
He can hardly get away or control his horse.

HENRY. There you have the measure of these people.
You can labour night and day to give them
A world that's comprehensible.
But their idolatry goes to any man—
Though he reeks of fault and cares less about their lives
Than he does for a point of heresy so fine
It wouldn't shake a hair in God's nostril—
So long as they think he bargains with a world beyond them.
Well, let them have his blessing,
Drawn with two fingers on the air.
I shall still bless them better in their daily lives;
And God can hear me and make the best of it.

Enter ELEANOR

ELEANOR. Other men have been busy with the ear of God.
There's news from Paris.

HENRY. Tonight he can lie
On his bed, and heave his breast with a sense
Of mastery which in fact is finished.

ELEANOR. Over how many years, I wonder,
Has Louis been pestering heaven for a male heir.
How many saints have been dragged from the calendar
To intervene? Almost a year ago

[51]

He lay flat on the chancel floor, refusing
To get up again until the Chapter had promised
To combine in one great assault of prayer.

HENRY. What is the news from Paris?

ELEANOR.   The power of prayer
Is the news from Paris. It has come in a letter
Written by Gerald of Wales three nights ago.
He was working late, he said, and had just put
His philosophy-fuddled head on to the pillow
When the frame of his bed began to shake
With a vibration of bells from every church in the city.
His dark room was all of a sudden
Staggering with torchlight. So he dived for his shirt
And made for the window. The whole of Paris was out
Streaming westwards. The prayers have reached their mark.

HENRY. It has taken them twenty years to get there.

ELEANOR. When he called from the window for news, an old woman
Waved a burning torch under his chin.
'Watch out for yourself,' she said,
'A king's been born in Paris tonight
'Who is going to be a hammer to your king of England!'—
So even the bricks and haycocks in France are dancing.
The child has got into their wine.

HENRY. They'd better make the most of it. He may die yet.

ELEANOR. They have called him Philip-Augustus, Dieu-Donné,
Given by God on an August night; hinting,
What's more, at empire, a name full of promise.
                    [HENRY *turns to the men of the* COURT.

HENRY. You can all go to your beds.
Except you, Marshal; bring Foliot here.
                              [HENRY *and* ELEANOR *alone.*

[52]

HENRY. You're pleased with the news from Paris.

ELEANOR. When heaven makes one of its rare rejoinders
I should have thought it the merest common civility
For all of us to attempt a smile.

HENRY. It's a smile against everything we've succeeded in.

ELEANOR. I smile however I am moved to smile.

HENRY. Even at the prospect of a troubled future.

ELEANOR. You haven't left my mind much else to do,
Except appreciate
Life's more acid comments on human endeavour.
And then I smile. Tell me, in fact,
What place do I have in your perfect order?
You served me, and your posterity is safe.
So much for you and me. And now I am nothing in this land,
Nothing but your occasional whore.
I have been a legend. What is left of that now?
You expect me to abandon
The inheritance of brain and heart
Which I received from my ancestors,
Who for generations have been a race of men
Born to act on events like sun on the vine.
But before the vows of marriage I accepted the vows
Of birth and blood. I shall be as faithful to mine
As you are to yours, though yours are lawless:
You who so struggle for order everywhere
Except in your own life.
If anarchy should prove to be a state which is indivisible,
Stretching from your own body across the face of the world,
You have stinging days ahead of you. Meanwhile
I smile, at this and that; and the boy born to France.

HENRY. The future of the young eagles means nothing to you.

E   [53]

ELEANOR. Does it not? I am their mother.

HENRY.   And I'm their father,
However at odds I may be with time and men;
However beset within and without, I am still
Their father; and your birth and blood
To which you say you intend to be true, mingle there
With mine. God above us, the house is a single thing!

ELEANOR. Though no man in the kingdom has enough fingers
To count your women: and all men know what tunes
You play on that Welsh harp, Rosamund de Clifford.
[*Sings to herself.*] 'By the flowing river a flower is growing.
'In a Thames bower gleams the king's own flower.
'Rosamunda, Rosamund, rose of the world . . .'
Curious I should forget how that song goes on. I hear it so
often, when the wind's my way; though usually whistled.
        Re-enter WILLIAM MARSHAL, *with* GILBERT FOLIOT.

HENRY. There's nothing to be said. The days are hot;
The thirst on the way demands a little shade
And fresh water. One thing I ask you to remember—

ELEANOR. You sent for London. Here he is.   [*Exit* ELEANOR.

HENRY. The labouring is most dark alone. Foliot,
There's a boy for France.

MARSHAL.   I told him.

FOLIOT.   I had heard.

HENRY. The scrap of flesh has given them a future.
France from now on has a new pair of eyes in its head.
We have to make sure those eyes look out on a future
Already decided, an established world.

FOLIOT. What man dictates the future?

[54]

HENRY. In this instance, I do. We'll put it in working order.
Young Harry can have the crown of England now.

MARSHAL. Two kings at once?

HENRY. We'll plant the saplings firmly in their place.
All the boys shall have their lands, and learn
To love and defend them while I am alive to see it.
Richard can have Poitou and Aquitaine.

FOLIOT.   The Queen's lands!

HENRY. Richard is the boy most hers; her lands
Fall naturally to him.

MARSHAL. Think a moment, sir; we know the young princes
Have a sight more vigour than experience.
What do you think they will make of a gift of power
Like this which you mean to give them?

HENRY.   Nothing but good,
Because the voice of Plantagenet is one voice,
Calling and answering along the same road.
The power I give them is trust and affection. How
Can this be ill spent?

FOLIOT.   Do you think the Archbishop
Will be prepared to crown the boy?

HENRY. What Archbishop?—It shall be done as I say.
Come on, we can discuss when and how. Do you see
The bated look the sky has? The way of the wind
Is altering. The trees are drawn with chalk on slate.
Spit in the air, Foliot. You will see how differently
The world looks in the morning when its plan
Is well drawn for a hundred years of peace.

                         [*Exeunt* HENRY *and* FOLIOT.

MARSHAL. But the morning was only another day. It emerged
sullen and bedraggled, after a night of bucketing rain, much as

we all did after a night of too little sleep. I heard the chanting of Compline, then of Mattins, and at last of Lauds. And the daylight was hard to face.

Enter TWO MONKS

1ST MONK. What is the news of him? How does he do, the Archbishop?

2ND MONK. He does very well. He has left us. So it goes.

1ST MONK. Is dead, do you mean?

2ND MONK. As far as the King's concerned, worse than dead. Last night one of the town gates was left unlocked, by the greased palm of a miracle. And heaven took the chance, and produced a storm of rain to cover up the sound of his riding away.

1ST MONK. He's out of the King's hands, then?

2ND MONK. Out of the King's hands, nearly out of the kingdom: disguised, heading for the coast; making for the French court. So it goes.

MARSHAL. Before noon the whispers had become a certainty. Before a month was over, Louis, to all Europe, was the man who protected the Kingdom of God, and Henry the man who was trying to destroy it.

1ST MONK. Thank God he is free.

2ND MONK. Thank God, if you like, for a father who deserts his children. That's the state we are in now.

1ST MONK. What are we to think of it, then?

2ND MONK. There is a toll to be paid to the devil on any road a man takes.

MARSHAL. As the day went on, the streets were choked with rumours. The man Becket was at large and the world rocked.—

But the King made his way as before, forcing new roads ahead of him. . . . There were other things to concern us. Today we've crowned the dark secret of the future. The young eagles are coming into their inheritance.

Enter BLAE

I was looking for you, sweetheart.

BLAE. Well, look who's here.

MARSHAL. I've brought you one of the new coins: struck to celebrate young Henry's coronation.

BLAE. How much more is it worth than the old ones?

MARSHAL. Not a ha'penny, but it's an interesting object. If you want to see them come back from the Abbey and take a look at your boy, I'll show you a place where you can squint through into the hall.   [*He leads her to a point of vantage.*

BLAE [*as she goes*]. Thanks. I'd like to see him again. How is he growing?

MARSHAL. Not altogether up, but he thickens; and what he hasn't got in inches he piles on in intelligence. He sits at his books like a man who would rather eat paper than beef.

BLAE. Ah, God, that's the strange thing! To think that though I never had a brain in my head I once had those brains in my belly.

MARSHAL. The King means to have him for his Chancellor.

BLAE. Well, you never know what will come of your guts.

Trumpets. Enter, as from the Coronation, YOUNG HENRY, GEOFFREY, RICHARD, *and* JOHN, *his brothers*; BLAE'*s son* ROGER *and* HENRY *and* ELEANOR.

MARSHAL. Here they come now.

BLAE. That's not him, is it? No, that's not him, I know.

[57]

MARSHAL. That's the young prince Geoffrey, Count of Brittany
by the new mandate. . . . And there's Richard: sings like a min-
strel: his mother's boy.

BLAE. There's Roger now; I know him, I know my boy!

MARSHAL. There he is. He keeps a dogged, patient kind of manner,
considering the provocation he gets from the four legitimates.

BLAE. He's a man on the way all right, God bless him. I didn't
do half bad there. That's a thought worth keeping to end my
days with.

[MARSHAL *leaves her and joins the Court. As the stage fills,*
BLAE *is lost to view.*

HENRY. So I've seen beyond my death; what other man
Can say that? Blessed to rest, if only for a moment,
On the days which won't be my concern. And then
It was good, that passing salute of the sun
As we came out on the street.

ELEANOR.   And the sighing silence
Of the crowd who saw it.

[*They go aside to disrobe.* MARSHAL *kneels to* YOUNG
HENRY.

MARSHAL. My loyalty, for all the days I live.

YOUNG HENRY. There's not likely to come a time when I shall
doubt it.

HENRY. Help him off with his robes.

YOUNG HENRY.   No; I'll wear them.

RICHARD. He has the illusion of being a king, Marshal;
Don't disabuse him.

YOUNG HENRY.   Brother Richard is having
A morning of envy.

RICHARD.   Says the shadow of his dad.

[58]

HENRY [*raising a cup*].
  A long and prosperous life to Harry, to keep
  The flower of the broom golden when I'm gone.
  Pledge him, Richard,
  And you, Geoffrey. John, the health of your brother.

RICHARD. Prosperity, if you can get it.

GEOFFREY.   And good endeavour
  To our wives, to hurry on the generations:
  Especially to mine. Much pleasure to Constance.

JOHN. I shall reign before your children.

GEOFFREY.   Will you, sprat?
  You mean to live as long as that, do you?

ELEANOR. A long life to all my defiant eagles.
                  [HENRY *sets refreshment before* YOUNG HENRY.

HENRY. May all men serve you well, and you them.

MARSHAL. Not many princes are given the dignity
  Of being served by a king.

YOUNG HENRY. If Becket had been there to crown me
  I should have known what my dignity was worth.

GEOFFREY. Good health to the troublesome Archbishop!
      [*A moment of silence. Except for a quick movement from*
      ROGER *towards the* KING, *no one moves, until the* KING,
      while MARSHAL *is speaking, swings round on the Court and
      dismisses them.*

MARSHAL. Each time he made a bold move to clear the way ahead,
  the ground became more dangerous than ever. When he thought
  he had finally disposed of Becket, the name of Becket was
  breathed out like fire all over Christendom. And now, when with
  love and trust, he stations the boys as sentinels to the Angevin
  world, the ground seems to crack where he stands.

YOUNG HENRY. Why shouldn't we speak of Becket. I am very fond
of him.

GEOFFREY. He does very well in France, I hear: hand-in-glove
with Louis.

YOUNG HENRY. They know how to value a man there, that's the
truth.

RICHARD. What do you put your value at, lord high brother? I'll
knock you down for a song.

HENRY. Good patience, do I have to plead with you
To think where your own interest lies?
Whoever makes harm for me harms you, and all
Those thousands of lives who look to us
For their safe conduct across time. We are bound
In one future, each depending on the others.

ELEANOR. And yet, you can no more make the future obey you
Than you can make yourself obey
Your own belief in the just mind.
Haven't you just driven out of your kingdom
Four hundred human lives, men, women, children,
In the middle of winter, out over a wild sea
With nowhere to go?—And their crime, what is their crime?
Simply their relationship to Becket.

YOUNG HENRY. Is this what he has done?

ELEANOR. They have gone to France, to spread the gospel
Of our just law-giving master of government,
To whose unknown fate my sons have been dedicated.

HENRY. To a strong peace in which they can thrive.

ELEANOR. You have set half Europe raging to see you brought
down.
I will tell you something certain about the future.
You will be alone. You have given my lands to Richard,

[60]

As though you considered me already dead.
It shall be so, then: to you I will be dead.
My life is in Poitou with Richard. There
At least, the warm sun will give me leave to smile.
And we shall make laws for sport and love
And put a little light in the eyes of Europe.

RICHARD. With three thousand men-at-arms at my disposal.

YOUNG HENRY. You caretaker of your mother's lands!

ELEANOR. You shall come to us there, Harry, all of you shall come,
Whenever you make yourselves your own masters,
Or when you need the sun to set your blood
Flowing more freely than ever it can here.

HENRY. That evil genius they called you once
Is alive again: turns now towards these boys.

ELEANOR. They shall show me how the world should be.
And I will believe there can be such a world.

HENRY. You were with me all through the time when I was shaping
The nightmare into an empire. Do you mean
To give the nightmare back to them? You can remember it.

ELEANOR. I know it still. But at last
I mean to wrench myself awake
And open my eyes to my own reality.

HENRY. Then please God you find that dawn less false
Than it is to me. Your true reality
Is in guarding what I have made.

ELEANOR. It's in myself, past, present, and to come.
Where will they find yours? They will break you open to find it.
[*Exit* ELEANOR. *The boys glance at one another.*

YOUNG HENRY. There are too many things wrong here
In the old world of your generation, father.

[61]

Hardly any content with the way things are going.
I have ears; I know what's going on.
> [RICHARD *gives a deflating twang on an instrument. There is silence for a moment.*

HENRY. Sons,
Look well into the human face.
You will see there the desert you must cross
If you mean to make the city. God knows
At first I could have believed all men
Were born of an act of love, though sometimes
To be contended with, or destroyed, or wept over,
Yet never altogether losing the trace
Of the good hunger which made them. Now there aren't
Many I can look at with much belief.
But, by Christ's blood, I'll give them the city of the law
Even if I have to make it by fearful means.
And then trust it complete into your hands,
Which are also of my making.
But first look well into the human face.   [*Exit* HENRY.

RICHARD [*strumming*]. 'So then they all to dinner went
                                     Upon a carpet green . . .'
Do Harry; visit us in Poitou
When your crown starts to cut into your forehead.

YOUNG HENRY. I can see it's been cutting into yours all day.

RICHARD [*leaning towards him*]. Now look again: a flawless brow.
[*He tips* YOUNG HENRY'*s crown.*] But what
Do we see here? It's the mark of the royal slavey.

GEOFFREY. Show him respect, Dick. You can still smell the holy
oil on him. Sing him the song you made for the coronation.

RICHARD. What is music to a man who has lost his liberty?
Well, we can try.

[62]

[*sings*]   To sing of a woman is no care.
          Only to mention breasts, belly, and thighs
             Is to have the music.
          Or sing of no more than her hair,
          The moist lips, the closing eyes,
             And there, there
             Are the words and the air.

          But praising a brother for a crown
          Which no more fits him than a basin,
             It's hard to do it.
          A shadow with a royal frown—
          What notes will fill the diapason?
             And where, where
             Are the—
                [YOUNG HENRY *leaps up and grabs the instrument.*

YOUNG HENRY. All right, I've stood enough!

RICHARD. Afraid of the truth?

YOUNG HENRY. Fed up with insolence and envy. I'll settle with
   you.   [*He takes off his crown and robes.*

GEOFFREY. Oh, this is excellent! There's war among us!

RICHARD. Less arduous than making songs. Look, what ferocity!
    [*They draw their swords.* JOHN *puts on the robes and the
    crown, which are too large for him.*

JOHN. I'll be the king.

YOUNG HENRY. I'm ready for you; come on.

RICHARD. Pleasure, pleasure, pleasure.
    [GEOFFREY *has also taken a sword, and is ready to signal
    the start of the fight.* ROGER, *who has stood silently by until
    now, suddenly speaks.*

ROGER. Don't be such fools. Put the swords away.

RICHARD. Ding, dang.

GEOFFREY. Their blood's up. Now we really have come into our inheritance. Mother Mary, this is very interesting.

> [*He starts the fight with a lift of his sword.* ROGER *gets between the fighting brothers. Unnoticed, he is wounded.*

ROGER. I tell you, you're not going to go on with this!

RICHARD. Look out, you bastard boy, we're busy.

YOUNG HENRY. Have you lost your senses? Get away from here.

GEOFFREY. Cut off his legs and continue.

YOUNG HENRY. Come over here, Dick.

ROGER. It's nothing to me if you want to slide about on your own blood.

YOUNG HENRY. Then get out of the way.

ROGER. Except that it's my blood too, at least in part,
But, aside from that, it's the blood of the whole body
Of Plantagenet government; of the world's peace,
And the outcome of everything the king has lived for.
What thought have you given to that? What other man
Living could have gone so ahead of his time,
Holding so steadily to what he believes in,
While envy, prejudice, and self-interest
Are disputing every step he goes? And now
You can't keep the peace among yourselves! I tell you
If you don't know how to combine in one Plantagenet will
You might as well trundle the crown straight into the sea!

RICHARD. We'll show you how we combine to deal with a pompous, impertinent ass!

GEOFFREY. Is the new King subdued by a cocky little bastard? . . . Look out.

> [*He has seen* HENRY *and* MARSHAL *returning.*

ROGER. I seem to have taken . . . a cut from the swords . . . when
I . . . [*He falls. The three sons, with swords drawn, stand in a semi-
circle around* ROGER.

YOUNG HENRY. It wasn't any fault of ours. He got in the way.

GEOFFREY. A burst of oratory knocked him down. Well, we're very
sorry.

MARSHAL [*kneeling by* ROGER]. Quite a scratch here; he's been
losing blood. All right, he's coming round.

HENRY. So you mean to carry out the prophecy:
From the devil we came, and to the devil we'll go—
Brother against brother, the sons against the father.
I thought we might have got free from that curse.

GEOFFREY. Nobody was going to kill anybody, as far as I know.
[RICHARD *goes off, strumming the instrument;* GEOFFREY
with him. JOHN *leaves the crown and robes beside* YOUNG
HENRY, *who remains.* MARSHAL *has helped* ROGER *to his
feet, but he loses consciousness again and* MARSHAL *picks
him up in his arms.*

MARSHAL. It's not so long ago that I carried him here
Struggling like a bat in a veil. No serious
Damage is done that I see.   [*Exit* MARSHAL.

HENRY.   But how much
That none of you see.

YOUNG HENRY.   What else could I have done?
Sit like a girl and let them mock at the crown?
They were trying to make a laughing-stock of me,
Said I was nothing but your shadow.
But I can make men follow me, and command them, too,
And strike fire out of my name as good as any
Or better.

[65]

HENRY.   You can find men to follow you:
   All the malcontents, hangers-on and family runts:
   They would follow you, if your brains were pig-swill.
   But if you want better than that, wait until time
   Has made something of you. As it is
   You're not fit to lead a crusade of children.

                         [YOUNG HENRY *puts his head in his hands.*
   Harry, have you never heard men mock at me,
   With a contempt for what I do, enlarging
   The errors, belittling the purpose, refusing
   To nourish the attempt; for all they're worth
   Increasing the chance of failure? When the world
   Laughs at its own opinion of you
   Don't let it destroy
   The man you are going to become.

YOUNG HENRY.   They shall see what I am.
   [*He takes his robes and crown and goes out, past* MARSHAL,
   who enters.

MARSHAL. He is in good hands. He will soon recover.

HENRY. I wish I could say the same of everything about us.
   But the days have been lamed, Marshal, somewhere in the mind.
   We may have to go on with that to the end now.
   Why do I see that arc of drawn swords
   And the falling body as though they would never leave me?
   Am I losing heart? Good man, that's not the trouble yet.
   I can go further and harder than we've come.
   But the health has gone out of the air.

MARSHAL. Sir, you remember at St. David's when you came
   To the great stone across the river, the woman
   Who screamed out at you Merlin's prophecy
   That the King would die as he walked across the stone.
   You hesitated; but you crossed.

[66]

HENRY [*chuckling*].   With my feet
    On Merlin's reputation. Right enough, Marshal,
    We shall reach the other side. You shall see
    How we change the look of things. The whole of Europe
    Is snarling at us, yes? Louis up in arms
    And off to invade Normandy, on the understanding
    That our day is over! Right! Now, Marshal,
    Observe the transformation. Henry Plantagenet
    Is in the mood for wooing. Our disturbing spirit
    Is prepared to humble itself,
    To cool the hot bellies, making such a gusty
    Rumble of indignation. Louis for a start:
    Catch him in Normandy, wake him up to see me
    There beside him, like his first shadow in the morning.

MARSHAL. Already he thinks you don't travel as other men do,
    But go on wings.

HENRY.   Carrying persuasion, I hope.
    'Why, Louis, my liege, this won't do.
    'I've brought sad confusion to your mind,
    'Which my sorrow will mend. You who know so well
    'The extent of divine mercy, will want to see
    'A reconciliation between Becket and me.
    'I promise him a safe return to England
    'And full possession of his office; and he can crown
    'Young Harry all over again, with his and your
    'Young Margaret.'—And so we steady the days
    And begin to cross the stone, Marshal.

MARSHAL.   And how
    Does the aggrieved heart of the Archbishop take it?

HENRY. Look, Marshal: I am going half way to meet him.
    And here we stand in Normandy, ready to float him
    Again towards England. And God knows I have shown him

[67]

Plenty of reverence—
Holding his stirrup for him while he dismounts,
Acknowledging that the less should serve the greater—
Louis could hardly do better.
And before God I would have things as they were.
I only ask him to treat me with tolerable respect
In front of these men who are watching us from their places.

[MEN *are standing behind. Enter* BECKET.

Let us show each other all the good we can
And forget our quarrel.

BECKET.   I am very willing.

HENRY. The days behind us are thoroughly rebuked.
If we ever remember them
It will be with such fierce pain, the days ahead
Will double their virtue to overcome it.
There have been many kings of England before me,
Some greater, some less than I am. And many good
And holy Archbishops. Behave to me as the most
Holy of your predecessors behaved
To the least of mine, I'll be satisfied.

BECKET. I am touched by this. Yet we mustn't forget
That if our predecessors had settled everything well
We should never have had to undergo
These fearful years, of such harm to us both.

HENRY. Maybe so. Also remembering
That providence is a great maker of journeys,
And whoever refuses to go forward is dropped by the road.

BECKET. At least I take hopefully to the sea with you;
And surely England will take us up
Like a palm-branch in its hand, to see us riding
Together again on the road to London.

[68]

HENRY. Well, that must wait till I come there.

BECKET [*a pause*].   Does this mean
I'm returning alone?

HENRY.   I can't come yet.
A little time will be yours to find your place again.

BECKET. This isn't the homecoming I expected.

HENRY. Your old weakness for riding in triumph, Becket.
I have to disappoint you. But if we go on soberly
The day for redeeming the past won't be far off.

BECKET. I pray it may come. But looking towards England now
Something tells me I am parting from you
As one you may see no more in this life.

HENRY. Heaven forgive us, do you think I intend
Any treachery to you?

BECKET.   May it be a long way from your wish.
But sometimes in the mind's despair
When every thought and contrary thought, every
Act and opposing act, equally bear some taint
Of the man I am, I see I may be one of those
Whose life won't serve.

HENRY.   Don't be too proud to live.
What's the matter with you? Can't you trust yourself
To accept the promise of things improving?—Becket,
The sea is running as smooth as a hound for you;
I'm sending you back with a pliant wind
All in your favour. And, if everything goes as it should,
You shall have the kiss of peace when I come to England.
Is this intention good enough to be blessed?

BECKET. In the name of Triune Majesty, the blessing
Of heaven on you.

F   [69]

HENRY.   And mine of the world on you.

[*Exit* BECKET.

MARSHAL. It isn't the blessing of the world he's after now,
    Nor yours; he is trying to find a success
    Beyond human argument.

HENRY.   Looking
    Into his eyes, Marshal, I could find nothing there
    Which could help us to a new beginning. He makes me despair.

MARSHAL. Thinking back on it now, he seemed to me like a man
    Who had gone through life saving up all passion
    To spend at last on his own downfall.
    What else are we to think, when we remember
    How he behaved as soon as he reached England?
    If that wasn't infatuation, that clumsy, aggressive
    Unforbearance, before his shoes were dry
    From the foam of the beach, there's no more charitable word.
    I shall never forget the Bishop of London's face
    When he brought us the first news of it.
    He came pitching to Normandy, like a leap to safety.

Enter GILBERT FOLIOT

FOLIOT. It has been even worse than I feared it would be.
    His rapturous welcome at Dover, and all the way
    To Canterbury, so buoyed him up,
    He might have been the lord of Spring
    Making his progress on the winter roads.
    Not a happy beginning to help him to moderation.
    And as soon as a roof was over him, he struck
    His note, in his most uncompromising key.
    Excommunication for all who took part
    In the crowning. And your men and his, my lord,
    Had already clashed with some loss of life even before I left.

[70]

HENRY. I put him in the way of peace.

FOLIOT. You will never have it in his lifetime!

HENRY [*raging*].
What's the good of any of you, standing round
Like a lot of rotting pit-props, while you leave me
Wide open to the insolence of a fellow
Who came to me first on a limping mule, and now
Might as well spread his buttocks on the throne?
Do you all intend to sit about for ever
With your hands hanging slack between your knees,
Leaving him to foul the whole distance we've covered?
Who will get rid of this turbulent priest for me?
Are you all such feeble lovers of the kingdom?
         [FOUR MEN, *silently touching and beckoning each other,*
         leave the stage.

FOLIOT [*disturbed*].
I may have spoken with too much bitterness.
My world is too recently shaken to see these things
In a prudent light, but that is what we must do
With God's help; as we tried, my colleagues and I,
To nurse him through the dangers of his temperament,
Hoping for wisdom. And in return for this
He cuts us out of the Church's body like tumours.
But I know I spoke with too much feeling.

HENRY [*cool again*].
And great relish. We can take to the counsel-table.
Consider soberly the best way to move against him.
He has made his last mistake, and exempted me
From any promise I made to forget the past.
As he insists on being the sickness of the kingdom
It's up to us to be the physicians, to diagnose

[71]

The sickness, consult, and cure.

[*He turns and sees the empty places.*
What has become
Of the men who were with us?

FOLIOT. I was half aware of their going, that's true, and felt
A passing fear that your words might have been given
A more violent meaning than you meant to give them.

HENRY. What words of mine? You have some damnable thought.
What the devil do you mean?

MARSHAL. You may have more devoted men about you
Than you knew, or men with a devotion
To work off some score of their own, only waiting
For the first excuse to show their love for the kingdom.

HENRY. But they have no love for me! Neither have you
To have let them go. They had no permission to withdraw!
This was your doing, not mine, Foliot.
Get after them, Marshal; set men riding
On every road to the coast, search every port
And ship, and bring the lunatics back
If you kill your horses!   [MARSHAL *and others hurry away.*
I swear before God
This wasn't what I meant! It was not what I meant.
Go and pray; have the pain of prayer
Harsher than you have ever known it.

FOLIOT. I'm convinced we shall see them back, my lord.

HENRY. Convince your knees to pray until we know the answer.
[FOLIOT *bows and exits.* ROGER *stands pale and still at the
extreme right of the stage.*

HENRY. Dear Christ, the day that any man would dread
Is when life goes separate from the man,
When he speaks what he doesn't say, and does

[72]

What is not his doing, and an hour of the day
Which was unimportant as it went by
Comes back revealed as the satan of all hours,
Which will never let the man go. And then
He would see how the natural poisons in him
Creep from everything he sees and touches
As though saying, 'Here is the world you created
In your own image'. But this is not the world
He would have made. Sprung from the smallest fault,
A hair-fine crack in the dam, the unattended
Moment sweeps away the whole attempt,
The heart, thoughts, belief, longing
And intention of the man. It is infamous,
This life is infamous, if it uses us
Against our knowledge or will.

        [The light is leaving the stage. HENRY *moves restlessly.*
I can hear the ice creaking on the river.
I could hear the horses on the frozen roads
In this taut air, half way from the coast.
How many days?

ROGER.   Two, my lord.

HENRY. They should have been back.
    Still have not come back.   *[He faces the audience in anguish.*
               Did not come.

    [He moves into the shadows. Enter a MESSENGER. *He does
    not see* HENRY, *and stands for a moment undecided. Then he
    calls in the direction in which he came.*

MESSENGER. You said I should find the King here.

VOICE [*off stage*].   Is he not?

HENRY [*almost unseen*]. Speak from there.

MESSENGER [*moving*].   My lord—

[73]

HENRY   From where you are.

MESSENGER. I've been sent to bring you the news from England.

HENRY. Be afraid. Be afraid to say why they sent you.
   You will never heal your mouth all your life long.
   Leave it to a man who's already incurable.
   I'll deliver your message.—It's the arc of swords.
   Becket is dead.

> [*The* MESSENGER *is silent.* HENRY *gives a deep, low cry
> from the darkness. Suddenly he steps into the light like a
> madman.*

   No men are fit to live, no-one in the world!
   Foul and corrupt, foul and corrupt. All
   Contagious. All due for death. Why should I spare
   A man who can bear life and bring its messages?
   They have made the King's name death.
   It is treason now to breathe!

> [*He has the* MESSENGER *in his grip as though he would kill
> him.* ROGER *goes to part them;* MARSHAL *enters.*

ROGER. This is useless, my lord, useless, let him go!

HENRY. Take him out of my hands, take the thought of him
   Out of my mind. There's been no news, nothing was said.
   It's only here in my head, it's only here
   Behind my eyes—only in my thoughts?

MARSHAL. No, my lord.

> [HENRY *turns and goes slowly away. At the farthest point he
> pauses, but does not turn.*

HENRY.   Let no one living come near me.

CURTAIN

END OF ACT TWO

[74]

ACT THREE

ACT THREE

HENRY

GILBERT FOLIOT

ELEANOR

YOUNG HENRY

RICHARD

GEOFFREY

CONSTANCE, *Geoffrey's wife*

MARGARET, *Young Henry's wife*

ROGER, *Blae's son, now Chancellor*

WILLIAM MARSHAL

A CAPTAIN

PHILIP OF FRANCE

OLD WOMAN

FOUR REFUGEES

SOME COURTIERS AND SOLDIERS

MARSHAL. For three years I watched him, living in his haunted
 mind. Three years, also, without a Queen: for the Queen was
 following her own fancies in Poitou, shaping her own dream of
 civilization. Alone, Henry tried to shake free of the shadow of
 Becket, going at last on a desperate pilgrimage of penance to
 Canterbury.

> [*The crypt at Canterbury, lit only by a few candles.* HENRY
> *is on his knees. The sound of monks singing the 119th Psalm.*
> HENRY *rises and sits on a stone seat against a pillar. He
> is barefooted, in a pilgrim's robe.*

HENRY. It may be the day's first mass they are singing.
 I can say the night has been crossed. Though you never know,
 Crouching in prayers in this holy cellar,
 Whether the light has broken
 Or the night's as dark as ever.
                    Enter GILBERT FOLIOT

HENRY.   Is it day?

FOLIOT. The first hour, my lord, yes.

HENRY. The monks still awake to aim their lashing.

FOLIOT. They're waiting for you, at the high altar.

HENRY. Come on, then.

FOLIOT.   Should I let you make such a penance?
 After three days of fasting, and twelve hours of vigil,
 How can the body endure this discipline of rods,

Two hundred or more strokes from these seventy monks;
And some, my lord, who saw the Archbishop's death
Will give the rod their memory.

HENRY. Let it take away mine. I've stood enough
Of this perpetual shuddering of the nature
Which makes each day the moment before judgement.
Three years of it, the grinding of the thought,
Rat's teeth on the bones of the mind.
It was never my guilt, only in the rage of words.
But, if I think so, I diminish nothing.
I accept it all, if I can be rid of it all.
They're welcome to take their toll on my flesh
If I can be free of the world's loathing, and my
Self-sorrow. In Christ's name, let's go.

> [*Exeunt* HENRY *and* FOLIOT.
> [*Darkness. The chanting of the monks suddenly stops. A pause.*
>
> [*Sunlight.* ELEANOR *with her Court at Poitou: the young
> queen* MARGARET; CONSTANCE (*Geoffrey's wife*). *Also*
> RICHARD, GEOFFREY, YOUNG HENRY *reading with his
> back to the others*, MEN *and* WOMEN *of the Court.*

ELEANOR. We are giving a new heart to the world
Here in Poitou, a new language for love,   .
Singers and poets with the tongue of Apollo,
Rivalling even France in the art of living.
We welcome Harry here, from the dark life
Of his father's kingdom. Here he will find the laws
Keep time in him like his own heart; for here
We govern as music governs itself within,
By the silent order whose speech is all visible things.
—But there is still business for this Court of Love.
How else can we define the world of woman
And man for you, before the Court adjourns?

[78]

COURTIER. Would the Love Court of Poitou consider
   That true love can long survive in marriage?

GEOFFREY [*to* YOUNG HENRY].
   You'd better give your attention to this, Harry!
   Will our wives be judging themselves or us?

YOUNG HENRY. I had a cool enough welcome from mine.

GEOFFREY.   You've been
   Away too long. The girl has forgotten the touch.

YOUNG HENRY. The whole enrapt colony of them
   Has forgotten what the world is like. They're asleep in the sun.

GEOFFREY. You seem to have overlooked the mind of our mother.
   She has a finger on every pulse in Christendom.

YOUNG HENRY. There's only one pulse in Christendom, the one
   Self-will, overriding everything: our father!

GEOFFREY. Ssh, quiet! They've come to a decision.
   This is interesting.

ELEANOR.   We are not unanimous.

GEOFFREY. There's my Constance!

ELEANOR.   Nevertheless, consider
   The nature of love. In love a man and woman
   Are newly minted as in the beginning of the world,
   Creating themselves out of each other's eyes.
   But in marriage, whatever world is made,
   Has the bones of the woman walled up in the foundations,
   No air to breathe, nor any light to move in.

GEOFFREY.   I reject the statement!
   No abatement of love in marriage, an increasing!
   And there's my wife, carrying for you
   The bulky demonstration under her heart.

CONSTANCE. You are called to order! This is contempt of court.

[79]

ELEANOR. It's a happy wife who finds love and marriage consonant.

YOUNG HENRY. Will you listen to what I have to say? Will you
listen?
In this drowsy hive you are all so in love with yourselves
No facts can penetrate. Do we mean to let
My father take all the world, and us with it?
At Canterbury I saw him whipped like a boy,
But, my God, now he has it all his own way.
However fast the rebellions come
Or the miracles flow from the dead Becket
They disappear like snow from the heat of his flesh.
At last I've got away from him: but if we mean
To have any independent life, we should listen
To what young Philip of France is saying. . . .

ELEANOR. There are murmurs of life still in this drowsy hive.
I have young Philip's confidence, and he
Has mine. Be with us here; you will come to know us better.—
Well, there we have the session's end.
Another day has gone ripening over the vineyards.
As the dew settles on the dust, contentment
Visit your evenings, and your sleep be untroubled.

[HENRY *is standing among them.*

HENRY. There is one more thing before you go.

YOUNG HENRY [*hysterically*]. If he tries to drag me back
To where I'm never given the powers that belong to me,
I swear I'll throw myself down from the walls
And finish what has never been a life anyway!

RICHARD. I've had no message that you meant to visit us.
Forgive us if we haven't a welcome ready.

HENRY. Forgive yourselves if I come like a man among enemies.

ELEANOR. It's my world that you step into here, Henry.

[80]

HENRY. I know this place of yours, Eleanor,
  Where you nourish whatever can do me harm,
  Where you corrupt the hearts of my sons against me,
  And knit your fingers with any man who hates me.
  I know your world, where an acid wit
  Is valued higher than the mind hurt by it,
  Where rules dictate how a man should move, or love,
  Or cough, or betray, or do nothing:
  The unexceptionable dance of what
  Has withered within. Where every syllable's
  Up for valuation by the code
  Of the best poets, and nothing speaks from goodwill.
  I have understood at last the truth of the text:
  A man's enemies are the men of his own house.

ELEANOR. A man's own house is what he builds for himself.
  Here you're in mine, which faces its own way
  And looks towards other things.

HENRY.   Not any more.
  It has come to an end. You are under arrest.
        [*The sons cry out in protest.* ELEANOR *sees* HENRY'*s*
        soldiers beside her.

ELEANOR. You take me back to yourself in the only way
  You know, by forcible possession,
  As you took your own vision of the world
  With a burly rape in the ditch. Your hopes, therefore,
  Are born bastards, outside the laws I recognize.
  The true law hides like the marrow of the bone,
  Feeding us in secret. And this hidden law may prove to be
  Not your single world, not unity but diversity,
  And then who will be the outlaw?

HENRY.   A fine secret law
  Which kills good faith among us! Yes, you can smile:

You think faith is a word I've no right to use.
But I can tell you, my love for women
Is more of a kind with God's laws
Than the aesthetic of adultery that you cultivate here:
And ever since Louis died
Political adultery with France
Is growing hot in all your dreams against me.
To which you add the violation of the minds
And hearts of these boys.
All this I'm bringing to an end.

ELEANOR.   You imagine so.
  You can accuse me of nothing, except of following
  The free course of events, the new order of things
  Which is growing up round us. You bring nothing to an end.
  You have kept young Harry breathing no air but yours,
  Sleeping, riding, eating, always in your presence.
  Is he any the more yours for that? He made
  His escape from you. And so did Becket.
  For what part of Becket, after all, has been done away with?
  Only his human failings. Now he is rid of them.
  His argument has become an incorruptible statement.
  Purpose, however wise, is hardly blessed.
  God thrives on chance and change.

HENRY. God use his eyes on me, this is sophistry!
  If Becket had wanted peace he could have had it.
  What's my crime? A secure Plantagenet empire
  And a government of justice. Am I to be
  The only man who goes begging for justice?
  And begging it from sons who will benefit the most.
  Affection they never lacked from me,
  Patience they've drawn on as if from a bottomless well.
  Let them try and deny it: and blame themselves

[82]

If I have to use harder means to make them know me.
[*To the* SOLDIERS:] Take the Queen to our care.

ELEANOR. You can drag me with you wherever you pace the earth,
Or leave me shut behind walls, you will know I am there.
Not I the prisoner. You, within yourself,
Are the one roped, waiting for punishment.
The shadows will only deepen for you. They will
Never lift again.
                    [ELEANOR *withdraws, the* SOLDIERS *with her.*

GEOFFREY. Haven't you forgotten the prediction about our family?
What it is our blood inherits? Each of us against the other,
Brother against brother, the sons against the father.

YOUNG HENRY. That is one hereditary right you can't
Deprive us of.

RICHARD.   You can't rob us of your nature.
                    [*Exeunt the* SONS. *The light changes. Enter* ROGER.

ROGER. Does a Chancellor, as fresh to office as I am,
Have a right to criticize his King?

HENRY. Any man has the right. But nobody
Can hit more painfully than my own thoughts.

ROGER. This is what I mean: this excess of grief
Against yourself is crippling your spirit.

HENRY. What did I do to lose them? First their love,
Then their lives? First Geoffrey, then Young Harry.
Geoffrey, a boy who spat with life
Suddenly by life spat away,
As though the fever said, like the voice of God:
'No more riding against your father.'
And then Harry, dying in a terrible anxiety
To have forgiveness. I doubt if a man
Can summon up enough grief to measure these things.

[83]

Enter RICHARD

RICHARD. Poor brother Harry. I have prayed that his soul
  Shall be well received.
  I imagine he is less perplexed now, taken
  To the fountain-head. I shall miss the thought of him
  Walking the world. I shall wonder about him.
  We'll say no more. Death forgives most things.
  I've come for your blessing, on my succession to England.

HENRY. You expect too much too soon.

RICHARD.   I only expect
  What's mine by matter of course. Unless you want
  To make it a matter of war. Do I have to show you
  By force that I'm first in the hierarchy?

HENRY. A wiser ambition would be to be first in my heart,
  A place you refuse to fill. But you have still
  One brother left. There is still John.

RICHARD. Oh, yes, there is still the favoured one!
  I can see a day coming when I shall find
  John has been conveyed into my place
  And England already disposed of.

HENRY. I dispose as I choose.
  By God, you'd better submit to my peace:
  And shall, till a world comes which I have no part in.
                                    [*Exeunt* HENRY *and* ROGER.

RICHARD. No, no, my father! Rather than that
  I promise I'll drive you back across your life,
  Town by town, over the road you have come,
  Until I return you to your beginning
  As lacking in power as when you were born.
                                    [*Exit* RICHARD.

MARSHAL. Ordeal by generation. This, then, was to be the end of
  the universal argument: the ambition for the world transformed

[84]

into private grief. Is he the man left following behind, crying out for justice, or the man living out his faults? I have no answer. I only know that Richard and young Philip together, drove us back town by town as he said he would. We fell back through the king's memories one by one. 'Here it was . . .' he would say; 'and in this place . . .'. But each time it was a grimace he looked at; he said so. The memory had been different. The streets were like furrows; or scars, rather; and we were driven out, leaving dead men slumped on the walls. Until at last we withdrew here, into Le Mans, the King's birthplace. A thick mist was over the valley of the river. We smashed the bridge, and as we started driving spiles into the fords the mist lifted. We saw the pavilions where Richard and the French army had spent the night spread along the edge of the wood only a few yards away from the river. When the King saw them, he turned to me as though to someone who should wake him from a nightmare.

A CAPTAIN [*entering downstage*]. Where is the King?

MARSHAL. Not far away. We shall soon have him with us. Stand ready.   [*Exit* CAPTAIN.
. . . He told us to fire the houses beside the river, destroy cover and hold the enemy back. But the wind veered, and the flames leapt roaring through the ramparts, and took hold of the city. The citizens have poured out through the gates, and here we are now, seven hundred men, fallen back to the fields outside the walls.
  [*Three* MEN *and a* WOMAN *come out of the burning city, pushing a handcart piled with their possessions.*

1ST. Will you come on? Your mother's dead, isn't she, and the fire's gone over her.

4TH. O God, God, blessed Mary!

1ST. Well, come on, then.

4TH. Where can we go?

1ST. All the rest of them's a mile on the road, aren't they? Tie the stubborn bitch to the cart.

4TH. Leave me alone.

1ST. Then will you move yourself? You'll see what comes to you when the French army's across the river and wants a woman. Walk, will you?

> [*They move on. As they go, an* OLD WOMAN *enters, struggling along slowly, dragging a feather mattress and talking to it.*

OLD WOMAN. Ah, come on. What's the matter with you, you old feathers? You're not going to stay and be burnt. You'll come along with me. I haven't dragged you as far's this to lie down on you. It's to save you from the roasting.

MARSHAL. Here, you can't manage to take that along, old mother.

OLD WOMAN. I ought to manage. They was my own gooses. It took me seven Michaelmasses plucking them. And the feathers flew up light enough then, when they was wanted in the bloody bolster.

MARSHAL. Is this all that you've saved out of the city?

OLD WOMAN. I've brought away a spoon in my pocket; but the rest this old dreadful fire he can have it. Because he's sure to have it, after. As long as I keep the gooses' bed. In the end, I've had my days pretty comfortable. But there's my dying day I haven't had yet, and except for these gooses under me there won't be no other company then. So they can stop dragging and come of their selves.

MARSHAL. I'll take it a bit on the road. There's a cart ahead of you. [*He lifts the bed on to his shoulder.*] Ah Christ, your damn gooses! There's some burning smudge got into me!

> [*He lets the bed slide to the ground, takes off his helmet and flicks away the smudge.*

OLD WOMAN. Won't you lift it up again? Ah, ah! How am I going
to do, if the old devil has got into my bed?
[MARSHAL *kicks the bed flat, and stamps on it.*
Is the old devil dead?

MARSHAL. May God do the same for the cares that scorch the King.
[HENRY, *dazed and half-blinded, enters from the city.*

HENRY. There's no more to come from God! I've seen what God's
mind is.
He knew I loved this city,
He knew if he ever looked into my heart,
He knew I loved the city I was born in.
And here my father lies in his grave. And I
Have thrust him in the fire.
I have burned my city, I have burned away
My own beginning, the one place in the world
Where memory could return untroubled, before
The earth began to bleed wherever I walked.
[*He looks up to the smoke-obscured sky.*
I meant the fire to save us! Do you think I kneel
To a God who can turn a brutal wind
To eat us up in fire? No,
I renounce all part in you: no such hands
As yours will have my soul. I'll burn it
Away like the city, I'll hurt you
In the centre of your love, as you do me.
Your eyes can sting like mine, and weep
With the same helpless water.
There's nothing left for either of us to save.—
We move out, Marshal.

MARSHAL. The men are waiting
Over in the meadow there, ready to stand or ride away.
All except Prince John. I thought he was with you.

[87]

HENRY. John not here? Damn him, it's a cool woman
Who can hold him down in this heat. But he'll be with us.
He's been close beside me all through these weeks;
He knows what has been endured, for the sake
Of his inheritance. How near have they come?

CAPTAIN. They're already wading the water, my lord.
Half Count Richard's men are across.

HENRY.   This time
He's not going to find a forgiving father, but days
Of riding after us till we make a stand
With the fresh troops of Anjou.
All right, sound retreat. And tell your men
No carrying away loot. This ride will find
The weak seams in all of them, men and horses.

Enter ROGER

ROGER. The people who have left the city have turned back on the
road.

MARSHAL. There's an old fording-place there if the French have
found it.

ROGER. The way out is getting narrower.

HENRY [*to the* CAPTAIN]. We'll go through the woods. Halt at the
first clearing.
I'll join you there.
            [*A trumpet call.* HENRY *is suddenly as gay as though he
            were a boy again.*
                        That trumpet will bring John.
I know every crawling root and low bough of these woods,
Hunted and roamed it all over in my boyhood:
Path, and turn, and brook, I'll show you the ways.
And we'll shake off Richard, leave him confounded.

[88]

Come on; the years are only beginning.
We head for Anjou; with Angevin men we can start again.
I turn my back, yes, I turn my back,
But when I turn my face—Marshal, Marshal—
Where are the horses? Get me into the saddle.

> [*He gasps with pain and grips the shoulders of* ROGER.

MARSHAL. Sir, we're ready; it's time to go.

HENRY. My own body now—my own body—

MARSHAL. What is it?

HENRY. —fights me. From the heels to the throat, Marshal!

MARSHAL. Lean on me. You'll crack the boy's bones.

ROGER. He can have my breath if it helps him.

MARSHAL. This is no place to stand. Walk these few paces. Come
on, sir. The miles of the world have been nothing to you.

HENRY. Ah! Almighty God!

MARSHAL. Once through this you'll be back to everything you were.

HENRY. You think so, good.—But you don't know this pain! It
hasn't—[*He pitches on to the gooses' bed.*] It hasn't a sense of
mercy.

MARSHAL. You can defeat it, we must ride away.

HENRY. Cannot ride.

MARSHAL. Cannot? That has never been a word of yours, my lord.

HENRY. Cannot. It's mine now.

ROGER. Both armies are coming up: one out of the smoke, the
other out of clouds of dust.

HENRY. Well, I'm here. And they come.

> [*He turns in agony on to his face.*

ROGER. Look how his breathing tugs him, Marshal.

MARSHAL. He must lie there, though we love him.

> [*A roll of drums from the left, answered from the right. The standard of Aquitaine is borne out from the city, the standard of France from the road. The clothes of the men are heavy with water.* RICHARD *comes forward, smiling, to* PHILIP *of France.*]

RICHARD. We've come through that action, Philip France,
Like sheep through a dip, sweating and red as fire,
Damp as the water, but unscratched. Not a man
To receive us. What sheep-faced fools do we look?

> [*He laughs, but* PHILIP *does not; his head turns, and his eyes rest on* HENRY.]

PHILIP. Henry of England. Henry of England.

RICHARD. My father, God be with me! We have brought him down after all!

PHILIP. I was born to meet him at this moment. Wake him.

MARSHAL. He hears you, and knows whose voice it is.

RICHARD. It's the old dog's custom to take his sleep waking.

PHILIP. Does he mean to feed himself into the ground
Now that his greatness has been so humbled?
Tell him the time for that hasn't come yet.
There are things to be said between us.

MARSHAL. He's in too much pain.

RICHARD.   He picks his time well.

MARSHAL. I'll come with you as a hostage; you can be sure
He will meet you tomorrow.

RICHARD.   I love him for this!
He can use the quick swerve, the double back,
The dive for home, better than any ball player.
But only Lucifer knew how to fall and then

[90]

Come back into a kingdom. My father is only
Demon by descent. But he made the most of it.

HENRY. If a son can make his tongue goad at a father
My body can be made to stand. You shall have your conference.
      [He tries to struggle to his feet, but drops on to all fours, and
      moves towards them in this way.

MARSHAL. Does this give you a pleasure you can bear?

PHILIP. Help him to his feet.

RICHARD.   He's playing for pity
Trying to shame us into leniency.
      [HENRY gets to his knees, and then stands, putting MARSHAL
      aside.

HENRY. Mind your own business, Marshal. Get it over,
You God-given boy. Get on with it.

PHILIP.   You have come
To the end of the proud years, when all events were Henry.
An old man now, with your self-appointed sorrows
To keep you company; no longer fit
For the care of the many people. The time has come
To make good the years of insult you gave my father,
As well as other men of worth,
Not least your son here. God with his gradual purpose
Has brought us face to face.

HENRY.   Spare us the piety.
What do you want?

PHILIP.   First of all the homage you owe me,
Placing yourself in my hands without question.
You will give to Richard: Poitou, Maine, Touraine,
Anjou, and Normandy.
Release his mother, your Queen, and call on your barons
To acknowledge him as your successor.

[91]

You'll pay an indemnity of twenty thousand marks,
For all the destruction of this campaign. Meanwhile
The castles which have fallen to us in this war,
As well as the castles of the Vexin, stay in our hands
Until everything demanded has been done.
> [HENRY *moves his head slowly towards* RICHARD.

RICHARD. This is all I ever asked. Except
For the indemnity, we make no other claims.

HENRY. All you asked. How much less is this than all?

PHILIP. The passing of years make their own justice.
> [*Still* HENRY *broods. The air is heavy and silent. Then a
> long mutter of thunder.* HENRY *raises his head.*

HENRY. Whose is this offence?
> [*A peal of thunder.* HENRY, *almost falling, is held by*
> MARSHAL.

Anything, anything. Stand back from me, Marshal.
And cover your ears. Further away. I am one
More who betrays the city.
> [*He turns to* PHILIP, *his voice very low.*
> You have my homage.
I can't get to my knees and up again, but you have it.
Everything you demand you know you can take.
That's done; the world has been altered; I can go.

PHILIP. We end the day with the kiss of peace, then.
> [PHILIP *gives* HENRY *the kiss of peace.* RICHARD *comes
> forward to do the same. As he kisses his father,* HENRY *speaks
> softly.*

HENRY. You have a lesson to learn. Death can wait
Until your brother John and I have made you
A fair return for this.

RICHARD.   My brother John?
And where do you suppose my brother John is?

HENRY. God forgive you. You've taken him prisoner.

RICHARD. Prisoner? John? My own dear brother? No.
He came over to us in the best of spirits this morning
To be on the side where the sun was rising.

HENRY.   Liar!

RICHARD. Brother John is allied with his brother Richard.

HENRY. He knows we undertook all this for him.

RICHARD. Who's for a rest, Philip? My throat's as rusty
As the earth here.

PHILIP.   There's a tent pitched in the field.
Water to wash in, and wine to swill down the dust.
Though in my spirits I could walk the world now.
                    [*Exeunt* PHILIP *and* RICHARD.

MARSHAL. Sir, sir, sir.

HENRY.   That's all, that's all that was left
To come. The rest can go on, on and on
As it will.

MARSHAL. Give way, sir; lie down here.

HENRY. Give way, go down . . . they all say it: go down,
Give way, go down.   [*He goes blindly on to the bed.*
            Shame, shame, shame,
On a conquered king.
        [MARSHAL *crouches beside* HENRY, *and makes a pillow of
        his cloak while he speaks.*

MARSHAL.   You're only obeying
Your own body's knowledge of endurance
Which says Hold still for awhile, raging man.
Hour after hour, for thirty years,

[93]

You have shouldered up a world towards your mind,
Seen it thrown down more than once
As though for ever, and righted it, lifted it,
Borne it even higher. It would have broken
Twelve men's hearts, each of your own strength,
To have hewn their way through these years as you have.
The severe day begs for a little night to rest in.
Only a bruised, not a conquered King.

ROGER. Sir, believe what you've accomplished.
Your laws are fixed on England: grumbled at
Like the weather, but, like the weather, accepted
As a source of strength. The people have become
Their own law, in the twelve men representing them.
Unparalleled in Christendom, this new nature of the island.

HENRY [*in delirium*].
Hot on the road, eleven furlongs from Paris.
And now we're carrying half of France, the horse
Has good reason to stumble.

MARSHAL [*to* ROGER].   There's the fever talking.
I'll find somewhere where he can lodge before
The sun goes down. And out of the sound
Of that triumphant mob of France,
Singing there in the field, like a village wedding.
                                            [*Exit* MARSHAL.

HENRY. The bells are ringing—do you hear them, father?—to
celebrate my marriage. We've got the lustrous Queen. We can
start creating the world. My sweat could lie with hers and breed
rivers. It's too hot to ride any further. I'll get down into the water.
There's my father, washing the filthy summer sweat off him.
                          [*He struggles to get out of his clothes.*

ROGER. Wait a bit, sir: your father's not there now.

HENRY. Yes, he is there. Father, stay where you are. I'm coming. The grime of the journey is fearful. We have to wash it off.

ROGER. It's all right, sir: there it is: you have had your bathe.

HENRY. No. By no means. I'm not washed clean. [*He shudders.*] The water's been lying in the dark too long. It's icy cold. The caked sweat and dirt goes in so deep you have to wash to the bone.

ROGER. You're well washed now. Feel the water on you.
    [ROGER *guides the King's hand across the sweat on his body.* HENRY *turns his eyes to him.*

HENRY. On our way from Paris we bathed in a deep pool away from the sun. At night my father lay like this; in two days he was dead. Do you know who I am?

ROGER. The King, my lord.

HENRY. And who is this man the King?

ROGER. My father.

HENRY. That wasn't thought of when I got you. A bull night and an unfastidious whore, while the rain soaked through the tent. And by God's mercy you were made. I've done better things and been worse punished.

ROGER. I owe you a life, sir.
    [ROGER *dries the sweat from* HENRY's *body with a cloth. Enter two or three* MONKS. *They stand beside* HENRY.

ROGER. Why are you standing here? What do you want?

MONK. We have come a long way to reach the King. We come from Canterbury.

ROGER. Christ Church monks: this is no time or place for you.

MONK. We have found the King. And what better time for him to feel the troubles of other men than now, when he knows

[95]

affliction? We have come for a grant of our rights. No one but the King can give us the justice we need.

HENRY. You must wait until I come to England. Don't think because you see me stretched here on the rack, you can extort unfair promises. I'll hear you when I return.

MONK. What sort of answer is this to men who have struggled five hundred miles to see you?

ROGER. You have heard the King. And you know he keeps his word. Go back to England, practise patience, he'll come to you.

[*The* MONKS *move away. One turns back, his face contorted with anger.*

MONK. By the merits of the blessed Thomas Becket, whose life and passion so pleased heaven, God will shortly do us justice on your body!

[HENRY's *head swings away, and he gasps.* ROGER *rises in rage, but* HENRY *pulls him down to his knees. Exeunt* MONKS.

HENRY. We have to hear it. I know this will never lift off me. . . . When you can, write for me to the Prior, tell him I think with concern of the difficulties which are his. Say that meanwhile they should consider deeply of the two sides, and think well of peace. Say they did harshly, to bring Becket out of the grave.

ROGER. Yes, my lord.

HENRY. You shall have this ring: the Plantagenet leopard.

ROGER. No, my lord, no. The leopard has to stay on your hand.

HENRY. It has bitten deep into my finger. There it is.

ROGER. I'll not take it until you are back to power, both in body and kingdom.

HENRY. Only you of the brood haven't confirmed that all my affections were a fool's errand. . . . What are you saying?

ROGER. Sir, I was praying that God would soon return you to prosperity.

HENRY. The decision's already been made. There's no argument any more, and no more heavy blows between us. Go and call back that monk who cursed me with such pleasure that it made him tremble. Now he can absolve and bless me for his trouble. The formalities of allegiance. I believe in the law.

ROGER. Time for that when we've taken you to shelter.

HENRY. Call him now; while he still remembers me.

ROGER. I'll go when William Marshal comes back, my lord.

HENRY. Are you failing in obedience?

ROGER. I mean I can't leave you alone, my lord.

HENRY. What's the harm? I'm familiar with this place. Fetch him.
[ROGER *rises and looks into the growing shadows where the* REFUGEES *are crouching.*

ROGER. Good people, while I'm away watch over him.
You know he comes of your city, and you of his.
Take care of him as a neighbour, and if he calls for me,
Shout as you run to fetch me; I shall hear you.
[*Exit* ROGER. *The* REFUGEES *move a little forward.*

3RD. You know, this was the king of the world, so men say.

4TH. He is looking.
[*The* KING *and the* REFUGEES *gaze at one another.*

HENRY [*in great anxiety*]. I don't know . . .

1ST. What, then?

HENRY. . . . if the laws will hold.
[*The* REFUGEES *gaze.* HENRY *turns his head away from them. A violence attacks his body. He tries to pull himself up.*
It is all still to do!
[*He falls back, and is silent.*

[97]

1ST. Mary Virgin, but I think he's dead.

2ND. Shall I put my ear to his heart?

4TH. No, come away. You can't come close to a great king.

> [*The* OLD WOMAN *is whimpering and praying.*

1ST. I wouldn't come close to a great king, but what we have here is a dead man. You've seen fifty like it or more. I'm thinking, we've had nothing from him yet, and he's lost us everything we had in this burning city. This dead fellow owes us a bit of justice.

2ND. But he's a dead man, so he doesn't pay.

1ST. Nor say No either. He doesn't refuse us. These things he has will only go to them who want nothing. For anyway he'll be stripped before they bury him, and washed and that.

4TH. I won't stay and see you lay hands on him.   [*Exit.*

> [*The* 2ND *has nervously joined the* 1ST *in stripping the body.*

1ST. This is gold, do you see that?

OLD WOMAN. It's wicked work, it's wicked work.

1ST. We'll give you something, but shut your mouth.

OLD WOMAN. I won't have nothing of it. I'm only waiting here to have my gooses' bed.

3RD [*on watch*]. They're coming. Run, man!

> [*As he runs past the cart he grabs some belongings.* 1ST *and* 2ND *take to their heels. The* OLD WOMAN *sits with the body of the* KING, *gabbling her prayers.*
> *Enter* WILLIAM MARSHAL, *carrying a hurdle; and* ROGER *with the* MONK.

MARSHAL. Mercy of God, look!

ROGER. O God in heaven! O my father! I should never have left him. I thought they were simple men, but they were devils. [*He turns on the* OLD WOMAN.] You sat watching this, without calling for help which would have brought me to him. Did they kill him before they robbed him? Which way are they gone?

OLD WOMAN. I told them it was wicked work they did, wicked work they did. But he died in his own time, before they came up close. He was dead when they came to him.

ROGER. They'll be brought back and made to suffer for it.

MARSHAL. It serves no turn. It was in his heart to give them a world. Help me to lift him.

[*They lift* HENRY *from the bed to the hurdle.* ROGER *takes off his velvet cloak and spreads it over the body.*

MARSHAL. 'Christ,' he said, 'we'll have no naked men.'

[MARSHAL *and* ROGER *carry* HENRY *away on the hurdle, the* MONK *following.*

[*The* OLD WOMAN *sits for a moment. She gets up and goes to the feather mattress, tugs at it, and begins to drag it towards the cart.*

THE END

PRINTED IN GREAT BRITAIN
AT THE UNIVERSITY PRESS, OXFORD
BY VIVIAN RIDLER
PRINTER TO THE UNIVERSITY